Training Peer Helpers

Coaching Youth to Communicate, Solve Problems, and Make Decisions

BARBARA B. VARENHORST, Ph.D.

SEARCH INSTITUTE PRESS

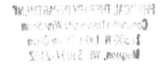

Training Peer Helpers:
Coaching Youth to Communicate, Solve Problems, and Make Decisions

Barbara B. Varenhorst, Ph.D.

Search Institute, 615 First Avenue NE, Suite 125, Minneapolis, MN 55413;
612-376-8955, 800-888-7828; www.search-institute.org

Editors: Rebecca Aldridge, Jennifer Griffin-Wiesner, and Kathryn (Kay) L. Hong
Design and typesetting: Nancy Johansen-Wester
Production: Mary Ellen Buscher

ISBN-13: 978-1-57482-490-2

Library of Congress Cataloging-in-Publication Data

Varenhorst, Barbara B.
  Training peer helpers : coaching youth to communicate, solve problems, and make decisions /
by Barbara B. Varenhorst.
    p. cm.
  ISBN-13: 978-1-57482-490-2 (pbk.)
  ISBN-10: 1-57482-490-2 (pbk.)
  1. Peer counseling of students 2. Student counselors—Training of. I. Title.
LB1027.5 .V2996 2010
371.4'046—dc22

                              2010031274

About Search Institute
Search Institute is an independent, nonprofit, nonsectarian organization whose mission is to provide leadership, knowledge, and resources to promote healthy children, youth, and communities. The institute collaborates with others to promote long-term organizational and cultural change that supports its mission.

 Search Institute's Healthy Communities • Healthy Youth initiative seeks to unite individuals, organizations, and their leaders to join together in nurturing competent, caring, and responsible children and adolescents. Lutheran Brotherhood, now Thrivent Financial for Lutherans, was the founding national sponsor for Healthy Communities • Healthy Youth. Thrivent Financial for Lutherans has provided Search Institute with generous support.

Contents

Session 9. Assertiveness Skills: Dealing with Peer Pressure   75

Session 10. Assertiveness Skills: Managing Sensitive Issues   83

Session 11. Confidentiality and Decision Making   97

Session 12. Decision Making as a Process   107

Handouts

All handouts can be found on the CD-ROM included at the back of this book

Introduction

Simply put, peer helping is young people helping other young people. Youth have the power to make a real difference in the lives of the people around them. When young people have troubles, frustrations, concerns, worries, or life events that affect them, they often turn to peers rather than adults for help. A peer-helping program teaches students skills that strengthen what they have to offer peers. Trainees learn how to effectively provide help, practical assistance, and support to those in need.

Peer-helping programs are not limited to schools. They can take place in after-school settings, community centers, youth organizations, congregations, sports groups, and even businesses that employ youth. Peer helping itself can take many forms. It may happen casually one-on-one, such as reaching out to a new student. It may occur more formally in peer-based programs, such as tutoring, mentoring, support, mediation, conflict resolution, counseling, and ministry.

THE BENEFITS OF PEER HELPING

Studies show that peer helping in its diverse applications is beneficial in many ways:
- As youth become peer helpers, they not only learn how to cope with their own developmental tasks, but also begin to recognize their own unique qualities, skills, talents, and experiences that can be useful in helping others (Varenhorst, 2004).
- Students who participated in a grade 5 peer-helping program reported gains in interpersonal relationships, academic performance, and personal characteristics, including increases in the desire to help others, self-confidence, and persistence (Larrier, Harris, and Linton, 2009).
- A comprehensive evaluation of peer programs in California found that life skills—academic achievement, self-esteem, connectedness to school and community, communication, decision-making/problem-solving, and conflict resolution/violence prevention—improved as a direct result of the peer program (Forouzesh, et al., 2001).
- A study of peer helpers who themselves were considered at-risk revealed benefits including a deeper sense of connection and interdependence with other people and a sense of responsibility to their communities (Quigley, 2004).
- A recent study of cross-age peer mentoring found an association between serving as a peer mentor and increases in academic connectedness and self-esteem (Karcher, 2009).
- The evaluation of a cross-age alcohol prevention program found benefits for both

elementary and high school participants, including increased knowledge of alcohol risks, less reported binge drinking, and increased teaching skills (Bell, Kelly-Baker, et al., 2005; Padget, Bell, et al., 2005).

- Researchers studying middle school students in peer helping programs in New York State found a positive correlation between participating in peer mediation programs and enhanced academic outcomes (Bogner, Gullo, et al., 2008).
- By having a positive impact on students, peer programs create a more positive school climate (Forouzesh, et al., 2001).

Most adults who train students in peer helping find it a stimulating and meaningful experience. This training will help you enjoy a similar relationship with youth. As a leader who genuinely believes in young people, in trusting them and encouraging them, you can be an important asset builder in their lives. Being a role model admired by youth is a privilege that should not be taken lightly. The job often demands hard work and careful thought, as well as the best and the finest of all of us who accept this opportunity.

DIRECTIONS FOR USING THIS GUIDE

You can use *Training Peer Helpers: Coaching Youth to Communicate, Solve Problems, and Make Decisions* to help any group of youth in middle or high school become peer helpers. The training involves 15 sessions, each approximately 90 minutes, which should occur in succession once a week. To make the training most effective for participants, limit groups to 10 to 15 members.

Any young person can benefit from peer-helping training. Young people of all types seek out the training when you extend an *open invitation.* When considering how to encourage broad participation, don't overlook "shy," "troubled," or "indifferent" students. In spite of how they have been labeled, these youth still have the qualities needed for trainee candidates, such as helpfulness, trustworthiness, concern for others, ability to listen, and potential to serve as positive role models. Ensure diversity in your group so that you can incorporate the asset of cultural competence into as many activities and discussions as possible. Once students have completed training, adult leaders can make the most appropriate matches for actual peer-helping tasks based on individual strengths.

Peer-helping programs require staff with the appropriate training to enable leaders to carry out their responsibilities. Please see the appendixes for the *National Peer Helpers Association Programmatic Standards and Ethics.*

THE PURPOSE OF THIS GUIDE

Training Peer Helpers: Coaching Youth to Communicate, Solve Problems, and Make Decisions is an updated and revised edition of my 1981 *Curriculum Guide for Student Peer Counseling Training,* which was written in collaboration with Pamela Toole and James Toole, coordinators of the Peer Counseling Program in Palo Alto, California. (Many of the activities and discussions featured in this guide also appear in a peer ministry version published by The Youth & Family Institute.) Much has changed in the nearly thirty years since the original training curriculum was published. Most programs referred to then as peer counseling now are identified as peer-helping programs.

This guide is the result of 32 years of training students and adult leaders throughout the country and observing and listening to the needs and problems adults encounter in being effective leaders. *Training Peer Helpers* is not a textbook for students. Rather, it is a series of lesson plans for adult leaders. It is intended only as a *model*—a model that you may need to adapt or supplement for use in different localities, with specific students, or for a particular peer-helping program.

Three factors have determined the guide's content: the purpose of student training, the methods used to conduct this training, and the importance of the 40 developmental assets in everyone's life.

This training is designed to assist students in learning to build helping relationships with peers. Many of these peers may be lonely, isolated, alienated, or socially handicapped in some way; however, all young people, not just those who are struggling, may at some time need to turn to someone. Students can use the skills they learn in this training to work one-on-one with young people they know and meet.

As opposed to a group counseling approach, the methods you will use in this training are *instructional.* Although students frequently use personal examples in activities and discussions, and at times may attempt to turn the training into a group counseling session, your focus is to *teach* the skills and build the developmental assets peer helpers need to be effective.

You instruct students mainly through group discussions, which allows for flexibility. Traditional teaching methods, such as lecturing, are less effective for this material and are not recommended. Adult leaders must be skilled group facilitators, making points in the discussions by calling attention to what students did or said while participating in the learning or practice activity. If you are not clear about what you are trying to teach, students will be unclear about what they are supposed to learn.

The sequence of training enables students initially to learn what peer helping is, which leads to the first basic skill taught—how to start a conversation with people you don't know. Each training session in turn deals with a new skill or different topic and builds on what the students have learned in earlier sessions. If students have not acquired the previous skills, they will have difficulty developing subsequent ones. Therefore, it is important to observe and evaluate students as they participate in activities. Concentrate on teaching each skill thoroughly rather than trying to go through the guide in a set number of weeks. Some skills learned well will be beneficial to students and reinforce their effort at peer helping, even if the total material is not covered.

The training's design enables the students gradually to build a cohesive, trusting group. With each session, the content progresses from general, less threatening material to more personal matters. If group cohesiveness has not developed, leaders will find it difficult in later sessions to get the group involved, making the training less effective.

Be sure to *prepare* before each session by studying it ahead of time and thinking through which questions you want to use, how you will introduce each activity, what additional thoughts or questions you might address, and how you will model asset-building principles. Also, ensure that you've assembled the necessary materials to distribute to students. You will find it especially helpful to review the Notes for Leaders that conclude each session. These sections provide suggestions for handling incidents that may arise, points to emphasize, and alternative ideas for activities.

SESSION CONTENTS

The first sessions help young people hone relationship-building skills so that they can better *understand* peer helping and *prepare* for gaining more advanced skills necessary for peer "counseling" and peer mediation, which they'll learn in Sessions 13 and 14.

Most sessions include the following key elements:
- Homework review
  The homework is designed to reinforce the material covered in each session. The homework review adds value to the assignment in that everyone learns from the experiences of others. The review provides an opportunity to model listening to youth and calling on them as resources.
- Summary of the previous session and introductory discussion of topic
  The summary reminds students of what you covered and provides you with feedback on how well the students absorbed the lesson and what you need to review or repeat.
- Learning activity
- Homework assignment
- Return, collection, and distribution of thought cards
- Reflection on assets

Some sessions also include an activity for you or a few students to demonstrate. At times, it is important for you to demonstrate or go first in the activity; at other times, it is important that you *do not*. Going first can demonstrate your willingness to share something personal and gives group members ideas for what you want them to talk about. For some activities, however, your going first could prejudice the information students decide to share. Each session recommends when the adult leader goes first.

The detailed sequence of events within each lesson and discussion is only a suggestion, and you need not strictly adhere to it. In fact, once the group starts talking, some flexibility will be necessary to promote discussion and accomplish the session's purpose. The guide also includes examples of what you might say to the group, but these too are only models. Instead of reading them aloud, you can supply your own words and personal experiences.

One session is structured to guide youth in thinking about their mission and their sense of purpose as peer helpers. Also included are two sessions on peer mediation. Currently, many programs are identified as peer mediation programs rather than peer-helping programs. However, peer mediation is one service, among many, that peer helpers can perform after they have learned the basic peer-helping skills.

The recurring "thought card" activity is another highlight that guides youth to deeper, more meaningful self-reflection about their values, decisions, perceptions, skills, and talents, as well as the assets they are building and strengthening. The personal observations assignment in Session 3 strengthens the vital interpersonal skill of observation and provides feedback on how others see and consequently respond to individual behavior.

THE DEVELOPMENTAL ASSETS FRAMEWORK

A feature that enriches this training is the incorporation of Search Institute's framework of developmental assets, the positive experiences and qualities that help youth succeed. These assets, spread across eight broad areas of human development, have the power to promote positive behaviors as well as counteract deficit behaviors during critical adolescent years, helping youth to become caring, responsible adults.

The developmental assets framework and its supporting research fit in easily with the basic training peer helpers need. Using an asset approach helps you create an asset-rich environment of caring, support, respect, and modeling that is shared between you and the students as well as among the students themselves.

Building assets for and with trainees enhances their ability to be effective peer helpers and to develop positive relationships. In turn, the training and the peer-helping skills it teaches can help young people build many assets and strengthen those they already have.

This training helps you build assets for and with your students in numerous ways. You start by becoming familiar with the assets and their meanings. Then through the sessions and homework, students learn the skills that build assets, reflect on their lives in terms of the assets, and collect ideas of how they can work with others to build these assets. The new feature of having young people help conduct lessons encourages leadership skills, which builds assets such as youth as resources and self-esteem.

Leaders must understand the 40 assets so that they can acknowledge them whenever students are demonstrating or implementing them either in or between training sessions.* Leaders must also be asset-building role models and be skilled in building relationships with youth.

*To learn more about the 40 developmental assets, see *The Asset Approach* or one of many other resources available from Search Institute, 800-888-7828, www.search-institute.org.

THE BENEFITS OF ASSETS IN TRAINING PEER HELPERS

Including the developmental assets framework in training has many benefits. Young people:

- Learn skills for caring and creating healthy relationships;
- Grow by nurturing their own assets;

- Establish a foundation (self-confidence, relational skills) for leading activities in their community, school, and organizations; and
- Develop skills, attitudes, and values that prepare them for positive relationships and contributions throughout their lives.

Additionally, when groups of young people are trained together, they develop a strong sense of community and mutual accountability and trust that enriches their schools, organizations, and other settings. For example, peer-helping training enables students to become change agents who can improve school climate. Caring school climates, in which the environment is conducive to learning, not only have healthy adult-student relationships, but also caring, supportive student-student relationships.

REFERENCES

Bell, M. L., Falb, T., & Roberts-Gray, C. (2005). Protecting You/Protecting Me: Evaluation of a student-led alcohol prevention and traffic safety program for elementary students. *Journal of Alcohol and Drug Education, 49* (1), 33–53.

Bogner, R. G., Salvadore, F., & Manley, E. (2008). The effects of peer mediation programs on middle school academic performance. *Perspectives in Peer Programs, 21* (2), 59–68.

Being an Asset-Building Trainer

"Walking your talk" is important as you teach these training sessions. The developmental assets framework offers the opportunity to lead students in a manner that illustrates the main principles of asset building. The following ideas, organized according to the eight categories of developmental assets, are ways to create asset-rich training sessions.

Support
- Greet group members warmly and openly as they enter the room.
- Create a caring, encouraging learning environment by consistently finding ways to facilitate relationship building among participants.
- Encourage students to seek information and counsel from one another.
- Regularly ask participants how they're doing and what they need.
- Be intentional about giving students recognition, encouragement, and approval throughout the sessions.

Empowerment
- Invite participants to be in charge of their own needs.
- Create a safe environment—encourage participants to move beyond their "comfort zone" in meeting new people and sharing ideas with others.
- Recognize and acknowledge each person as a resource to the whole group.
- Ensure that all students feel valued throughout the training.

Boundaries and Expectations
- Start and end the sessions on time.
- Be clear regarding the goals and objectives of the training and the degree to which participants' expectations will be met.
- Set clear ground rules regarding mutual respect and confidentiality among participants and intervene to protect participants when the ground rules are violated.
- Treat students as change agents and hold them to high expectations regarding session participation and post-session follow-through.

Commitment to Learning
- Understand and be responsive to participant's multiple learning styles.
- Demonstrate enthusiasm and curiosity for the subject matter.
- Be open to your own learning during sessions.
- Affirm students as a major resource in the room and encourage peer learning.
- If you are unable to answer a question, admit it. If students consider the

Forouzesh, M., Grant, K., & Donnelly, M. (2001). *Comprehensive evaluation of peer programs.* Pasadena, CA: California Association of Peer Programs.

Karcher, M. (2009). Increases in academic connectedness and self-esteem among high school students who serve as cross-age peer mentors. *Professional School Counseling, 12* (4), 292–299.

Larrier, Y. I., Harris, S. M., & Linton, J. M. (2009). Promoting student strengths in a strengths-enhancing environment through an elementary peer helping program: A one-year effectiveness study. *Perspectives in Peer Programs, 22* (1), 30–51.

Padget, A., Bell, M. L., Shamblen, S. R., & Ringwalt, C. (2005). Effects on high school students of teaching a cross-age alcohol prevention program. *Journal of Drug Education, 35* (3), 201–216.

Quigley, R. (2004). Positive peer groups: "Helping others" meets primary developmental needs. *Reclaiming Children and Youth, 13* (3), 134–137.

Varenhorst, B. B. (2004). Tapping the power of peer helping. *Reclaiming Children and Youth: The Journal of Strength-based Interventions, 13* (3), 130–133.

question to be important, decide with them how to find the answer.

• Share pertinent resources for learning.

Constructive Use of Time

• Be prepared and organized.

• Keep the group size appropriate.

• Stick to the agenda.

• Be responsive to the energy level of the group and be prepared to add quick energizers if they are needed.

Social Competencies

• Be available for informal interactions.

• Welcome and affirm the value of diversity with the group. Listen for and challenge comments that reflect stereotypes based on race, class, gender, or sexual orientation.

• Work to ensure the involvement of all students and adjust activities if necessary to accommodate those who may be physically challenged.

• Acknowledge and openly address conflict.

• Reinforce and model effective listening skills.

Positive Values

• Demonstrate care and concern for others.

• Value all participants equally regardless of race, class, gender, sexual orientation, or other differences.

• Do not tolerate jokes or comments that are put-downs of other people based on perceived differences.

• Act with integrity. Do what you say you'll do and freely admit it when you don't.

• Model restraint and healthy values regarding alcohol, tobacco, and other drug use. Be conscious of inappropriate messages that may be sent to participants when jokes, stories, or other banter involve sexuality or substance use.

Positive Identity

• Make yourself known. Tell your own story and affirm the stories of others.

• Maintain a positive attitude with all participants.

• Be open to students' concerns and possible resistance.

• Celebrate your own learning and the learning of others.

Adapted from *Integrating Assets into Congregations: A Curriculum for Trainers* (Minneapolis: Search Institute, 2000) and *Essentials of Asset Building: A Curriculum for Trainers* (Minneapolis: Search Institute, 2002).

Icon Key

 You'll see this icon whenever an activity is to take place during the session.

 This icon indicates items that need your attention in the session.

 When a discussion is to take place among the group, you will see this icon in the margin.

 You will know when to distribute handouts and other information when this icon appears.

 This icon alerts you to pertinent background information that you will need to review before sharing it with students.

 The appearance of this icon highlights points to make with students about certain activities or discussions.

 You'll see this icon when there is text to read directly to students.

 This icon appears when students need to direct part of the session.

Becoming a Peer Helper

Leader's Goals
1. To define "peer helper"
2. To help students feel a sense of belonging to the group
3. To help students understand the need for confidentiality
4. To work with students to establish group guidelines
5. To introduce the 40 developmental assets

Students' Skill Development
1. Learning names of group members
2. Learning about confidentiality
3. Observing—the skill of "listening with your eyes"
4. Establishing group guidelines

Leader's Tasks
1. To introduce the importance of confidentiality
2. To demonstrate the skill of observation
3. To explain homework assignments
4. To ask group members to bring a notebook to use as a journal throughout the training

Materials Needed
1. An index card (3 x 5 inches) for each group member
2. Flip chart and easel
3. A copy of the handout describing the 40 developmental assets (available in English, Spanish, and French) for each group member

INTRODUCING THE TRAINING

Start the training by asking questions that will help make the group more comfortable as well as give you some information about the participants:
1. What interested you in taking this training?
2. What do you hope to gain from this experience?
3. What is your understanding of peer helping?

Don't push group members for answers, but try to draw out responses. Then give a brief explanation of what peer helping is and what group members will be learning. Don't go into detail because they are not ready to process much information. A suggested explanation might be:

All of you know about the kinds of issues you and your classmates encounter at home, at school, and in your communities. You probably have thought about what you need to help you either avoid these issues or deal with them. However, you may not have thought of your own tremendous power as a resource in helping others cope with this period of life. You have the power to prevent problems, to help resolve them, to assist others who need help in various ways, and to provide feelings of worth and acceptance to your friends and other peers. Learning how to develop and exercise this power is the focus of this training.

INTRODUCING GROUP MEMBERS

Ask each person to give her or his full name, *including* a middle name, and to talk about her or his name. How do group members feel about their names? What nicknames have the students had? Do they know where their names came from? What funny experiences have they had because of their names? What different names might they have liked to have had?

As the leader, you start the process. In talking about your name, use as many different examples as you can to give the group ideas of what to say. Include nicknames, funny stories connected with your name, and your racial, cultural, or ethnic heritage as examples. You probably will say much more than group members will, but the extent to which you share will encourage them to say more by stimulating ideas for what they might say.

Tell the group how you would like to be addressed during this training, whether by your first name, Mr., Ms., Mrs., and so forth. Young people won't automatically know what to call you as an adult leader.

When you have finished discussing your name, start the sharing by choosing someone to go next, rather than going around the circle. Tell the person you select that he or she will decide who goes next. This process will continue until everyone has shared.

If some group members seem shy or only talk briefly about their names, ask leading questions such as: Where did you get your name? What is your middle name? What names do your brothers and sisters have?

Processing the Activity

When all have shared, elicit reactions to the activity by asking questions such as the following:
1. What were your thoughts or feelings about doing this activity?
2. What was easy or hard in talking about your name?
3. What did you learn about yourself by talking about your name?
4. What did it feel like to be the last person called on?
5. What kinds of names, other than your real name, do people call you in your school or in other social settings?

6. Generally, are these positive or negative names for you?
7. What effect does a positive name have on you or others?
8. How do you think negative names make another person feel?
9. How do you feel about yourself when you call another person by a negative name?
10. What feelings do you have when someone remembers your name?
11. Have you ever been called by the wrong name? If so, how did that make you feel?
12. How do labels and nicknames affect how you feel about yourself?

When finished with this processing, ask members of the group to try to name each person in the circle. Acknowledge the difficulty of this task, but urge some to try. Remind students that when you remember and acknowledge someone by name, you are helping to make that person feel important.

CONFIDENTIALITY

In talking about names, everyone has shared something about her- or himself. This provides a good opportunity to talk about confidentiality. Explain that two essential qualities for peer helpers are trustworthiness and being able to keep a confidence. Ask group members to define the word *confidentiality*. What does it mean to keep a confidence? If no one mentions it, point out that under the rules of confidentiality, anything personal someone shares with them is not theirs to tell others. Ask: Have any of you had a friend break a confidence you had entrusted to her or him? How did that make you feel? How did you handle the situation?

Although group members may not think anything "personal" has been shared while they talked about their names, emphasize that everything everyone said *is* personal and must be held in confidence; no one may discuss any of it with anyone, including their family and members of the group outside the training session. Perhaps someone has mentioned an embarrassing nickname or a middle name he or she doesn't like. Use these as examples, pointing out that it would be a breach of confidentiality if anyone talked about someone's name outside the group or used the nickname to address the group member in front of others.

Confidentiality is crucial, both in friendships and in this program. Some issues, however, *must* be shared for the safety of people involved. For example, students may have a friend who they think is being physically abused. This is a serious matter that peer helpers should report. Helping students understand and recognize this distinction is important. Explain that you will address confidentiality more specifically in future sessions, but for now it is significant to recognize that at times they may have to make a judgment about whether to keep a confidence.

INTRODUCING THE SKILL OF OBSERVING

After talking about names and confidentiality, introduce **observation**—the ability to listen with your eyes. This skill is important to a peer helper's effectiveness, particularly in picking up clues related to such issues as suicide, depression, and alcohol and other drug abuse—problems about which people often keep silent.

Peer helpers need to be skilled observers for two reasons:
1. Significant information often is communicated nonverbally rather than verbally. When we talk, we often make a conscious effort to screen our words. Most of us, however, do not screen the nonverbal messages we send, so they may convey a more honest or accurate meaning. Frequently, our bodies express feelings we can't express verbally. Therefore, to understand a person's real message, we need skill in paying attention to nonverbal cues.
2. Whether consciously or unconsciously, we are always observing others. On the basis of these observations, we make interpretations and expect individuals to act or respond based on these interpretations, or judgments, which often are not accurate. However, if we share our assumptions with the other person, we can correct inaccurate feelings or attitudes and then give helpful feedback to the one being observed.

Paying attention to nonverbal cues is like holding a mirror up to someone else. We reflect back the behaviors that we see and perhaps our interpretations of those behaviors. Such feedback may be as helpful to the other person as it is to us, particularly in understanding possible responses that person may get from others. Effective observations include the following:
1. A description of the specific behaviors one person has noticed about the other. Example: "Both of you were leaning forward, using hand and body motions."
2. Nonjudgmental descriptions. Rather than saying, "I observed that you were having a 'good' conversation," a peer helper should aim to state only: "I noticed that you were facing one another, and you both smiled a lot and were not distracted when I walked by. Based on this I assumed you were involved in what you were sharing." Positive as well as critical words carry judgments. "Good" conveys a judgment. Stating the behavior and following it by an interpretation helps eliminate any kind of judgment.

 To illustrate what it means to observe nonverbal cues, share what you saw as each person talked about her or his name. Point out that you were looking for behaviors that might affect interpersonal relationships and that could be changed if the person observed chose to do so. **Always give those whom you have observed publicly a chance to respond to your observations, either with explanations, corrections, or questions.**

Tell the group that to practice this skill each person will assume the role of observer at different times during training activities. Also, explain that at the next session you will assign each member someone in the group to observe throughout the training.

ESTABLISHING GROUP BOUNDARIES AND EXPECTATIONS

Given the sensitive nature of the content and skills you are teaching in this training, you need to set some rules that govern confidentiality, establish trust, and guide interactions within the group based on respect and the dignity of each person.

It makes a great difference in effectiveness if the group decides on its own guidelines rather than having the leader dictate them. Guidelines established and agreed on by the group send the message that each person counts and is trusted. Members are more likely to understand the guidelines and more likely to feel personally responsible to follow decisions that they have helped make.

One method for setting guidelines was developed by Linda Rosenblum, a peer-helping consultant in Wilmette, Illinois. To follow this method, hand out an index card to each person. Ask group members to think of a good friend, someone they can count on. What is it about this person that makes her or him a good friend? On one side of the card, ask students to write down the things the person does to be a good friend to them. Write specific behaviors, such as, "When I tell him something, I know he won't spread it around." Allow about five minutes for this.

Then have group members think of things that their friends do that bother them. On the other side of the card, ask them to write as many of these specific behaviors as they can in the next five minutes.

On the flip chart, make two columns: **Things Friends Do That I Like** and **Things Friends Do That Bother Me.** Go around the circle, asking each person in turn to volunteer one thing that a good friend does. Write these on the chart as they are given. Then ask students to volunteer things that bother them and record these. Review the lists and ask if anyone wants to add to either of them. Examples of these lists might be:

THINGS FRIENDS DO THAT I LIKE	THINGS FRIENDS DO THAT BOTHER ME
• When I tell them something they don't spread it around.	• They tell my secrets to others.
• They show up when they say they will.	• They ignore me when someone else is around.
• They listen to me.	• They tease people.
• They believe in me.	• They think I can't do anything right.
• They keep me from doing something stupid.	• They get me into trouble.

After studying the list ask the group to reword both the positive and the

negative behaviors as guidelines for group members' behavior. Based on these lists, the reworded guidelines might be:
- Keep things confidential.
- Attend each session because your presence is important and everyone counts.
- Listen. Do not interrupt.
- Respect the feelings of others. Do not put others down.
- Recognize when others do well.
- Encourage others to try.
- Be a good role model for others.

Create a list of behaviors that group members can agree are important to all. This list becomes the guidelines for how the group will work together over the course of the training. Hang this list where it will be visible during every training session.

From time to time, review the ground rules. Ask the group if any changes or additions are needed.

REFLECTING ON ASSETS

To begin the discussion on developmental assets, ask students, "What does the word *asset* mean to you?" After group members have responded, explain that while they are training to become peer helpers they will be acquiring the positive values, skills, and qualities that they need to be successful and happy in life. These "good" things are what you are going to call assets throughout this training. You will talk more about the assets in the next session.

Next, reflect on how assets are relevant to this session. Have students think back to the discussion of names. Remind students that when we remember and acknowledge someone by name, we are helping to make that person feel important, and that contributes to her or his developmental assets, such as the asset of self-esteem.

Move on to focus on confidentiality and the assets it introduces—honesty, integrity, caring, and responsibility. Talk about the meaning of each of these assets and ask: How might honesty and confidentiality seem to conflict?

Talk about the skill of observation and how it contributes to building inter-personal competence.

Setting group guidelines together helps students develop boundaries-and-expectations assets. You may want to share with the group the metaphor that life is like climbing a mountain and high expectations are the peak. Boundaries are the things, such as a map or road signs indicating danger-ous curves or falling rock, that give you context for how best to go safely up the road toward those high expectations.

Ask group members what kinds of ground rules or boundaries are practiced in their classes and homes. How does establishing boundaries make a difference in how they learn or live?

Using students' answers to these questions, talk about the asset category boundaries and expectations. Boundaries are guides or maps that teach students how to live and work together cooperatively; how to relate to others in positive ways; how to avoid arguments; and how to learn discipline that helps them avoid negative consequences. Ask how group members could help establish boundaries in their classes or homes if they don't exist.

Show the interconnection between assets by explaining that taking responsibility for following boundaries demonstrates possession of several of the positive-values assets, such as caring and responsibility.

Point out that the behaviors listed for good friends fit in with the developmental assets a person might want to build if he or she doesn't already have them. Ask: What behaviors would each of you like to work on to become a better friend? Distribute the list of the 40 developmental assets (Handout 1), and ask the group to say what asset the behavior relates to. Give students time to reflect and share, if they are willing. However, don't push for comments because the group members are just beginning to grow to trust one another.

HOMEWORK ASSIGNMENT

Explain to group members that at the end of each session you will give them homework to do, either to practice the skills they are learning or to experience new things that will enhance their peer-helping skills. Tell the students you will also ask for a report on their homework at the beginning of each session.

1. Ask students to find out the name of a classmate whom they have not yet met and to learn something about that person through talking with her or him.
2. Ask group members to talk to their parents or guardians about the names they were given. What meaning did their parents place on those names? How do parents feel about their own names? Did parents have nicknames when they were young?
3. Ask students to bring to the next session a notebook or something similar that can be used as a journal. They will be writing in these throughout the training.

1. The content of this session may take longer than one meeting. You can divide it by carrying over to the second session the Establishing Boundaries and Expectations activity. It is essential, however, to cover the name sharing, confidentiality issues, and observations in the first meeting. If your group is large, you can save time in talking about names by dividing into groups for sharing. Before dividing, have two or three members talk about their names in front of the whole group to set the tone and serve as examples.

2. Observing your group members while they talk about names takes a little practice. Sharing your observations, however, can be quite powerful. People seldom get constructive feedback about themselves. So if it helps you, jot down a few things to remember as each person shares.

3. If a student doesn't know anything specific about her or his name, suggest that a family member might be able to shed some light. How was the name chosen? Did the student have any nicknames? What can the student's parents or relatives tell the student about the family's heritage? Ask the student to share what he or she learns at the next session.

4. Guidelines established and agreed on by the group give the message that each person counts and is trusted in this training. Such perceptions are consistent with an asset-building environment.

5. The methods for creating class guidelines are only suggestions. If you have other ways for the group to define boundaries, use them. For example, you can also use the eight categories of developmental assets to come up with appropriate ground rules. Here are some examples:
   - Support: listen to each other; maintain confidentiality; build community.
   - Empowerment: be leaders and contributors; serve others through caring.
   - Commitment to learning: learn new skills; grow personally.
   - Positive values: show respect; be responsible.

   Once you have a list of ground rules, write them out on poster board and display them where students can see them every session.

6. Be sure to remind group members to bring journals. These will be used frequently.

7. In addition to passing out a list of the 40 developmental assets, consider ordering copies of *Me@My Best: Ideas for Staying True to Yourself—Every Day*, a booklet from Search Institute that introduces young people to the eight asset categories and encourages them to build upon their own strengths.

8. At the end of each session, you may want to debrief and ask the students what they thought were the positives and negatives of each session. Their answers can provide you with valuable information regarding what is working and what is not, so that you can make adaptations to the next session to better fit the group's needs.

9. You may want to consider passing out a folder to each student along with Handout 1 so that group members have a means of collecting and keeping subsequent handouts together.

10. You will need to prepare for the next session's observation assignment in advance. See pages 23–24 for instructions on how to set up and explain the assignment.

40 Developmental Assets

EXTERNAL ASSETS

Support

1. **Family Support**—Family life provides high levels of love and support.
2. **Positive Family Communication**—Young person and her or his parent(s) communicate positively, and young person is willing to seek advice and counsel from parent(s).
3. **Other Adult Relationships**—Young person receives support from three or more nonparent adults.
4. **Caring Neighborhood**—Young person experiences caring neighbors.
5. **Caring School Climate**—School provides a caring, encouraging environment.
6. **Parent Involvement in Schooling**—Parent(s) are actively involved in helping young person succeed in school.

Empowerment

7. **Community Values Youth**—Young person perceives that adults in the community value youth.
8. **Youth as Resources**—Young people are given useful roles in the community.
9. **Service to Others**—Young person serves in the community one hour or more per week.
10. **Safety**—Young person feels safe at home, at school, and in the neighborhood.

Boundaries and Expectations

11. **Family Boundaries**—Family has clear rules and consequences and monitors the young person's whereabouts.
12. **School Boundaries**—School provides clear rules and consequences.
13. **Neighborhood Boundaries**—Neighbors take responsibility for monitoring young people's behavior.
14. **Adult Role Models**—Parent(s) and other adults model positive, responsible behavior.
15. **Positive Peer Influence**—Young person's best friends model responsible behavior.
16. **High Expectations**—Both parent(s) and teachers encourage the young person to do well.

Constructive Use of Time

17. **Creative Activities**—Young person spends three or more hours per week in lessons or practice in music, theater, or other arts.

18. **Youth Programs**—Young person spends three or more hours per week in sports, clubs, or organizations at school and/or in the community.
19. **Religious Community**—Young person spends one or more hours per week in activities in a religious institution.
20. **Time at Home**—Young person is out with friends "with nothing special to do" two or fewer nights per week.

INTERNAL ASSETS
Commitment to Learning
21. **Achievement Motivation**—Young person is motivated to do well in school.
22. **School Engagement**—Young person is actively engaged in learning.
23. **Homework**—Young person reports doing at least one hour of homework every school day.
24. **Bonding to School**—Young person cares about her or his school.
25. **Reading for Pleasure**—Young person reads for pleasure three or more hours per week.

Positive Values
26. **Caring**—Young person places high value on helping other people.
27. **Equality and Social Justice**—Young person places high value on promoting equality and reducing hunger and poverty.
28. **Integrity**—Young person acts on convictions and stands up for her or his beliefs.
29. **Honesty**—Young person "tells the truth even when it is not easy."
30. **Responsibility**—Young person accepts and takes personal responsibility.
31. **Restraint**—Young person believes it is important not to be sexually active or to use alcohol or other drugs.

Social Competencies
32. **Planning and Decision Making**—Young person knows how to plan ahead and make choices.
33. **Interpersonal Competence**—Young person has empathy, sensitivity, and friendship skills.
34. **Cultural Competence**—Young person has knowledge of and comfort with people of different cultural/racial/ethnic backgrounds.
35. **Resistance Skills**—Young person can resist negative peer pressure and dangerous situations.
36. **Peaceful Conflict Resolution**—Young person seeks to resolve conflict nonviolently.

Positive Identity
37. **Personal Power**—Young person feels he or she has control over "things that happen to me."
38. **Self-Esteem**—Young person reports having a high self-esteem.
39. **Sense of Purpose**—Young person reports that "my life has a purpose."
40. **Positive View of Personal Future**—Young person is optimistic about her or his personal future.

40 elementos fundamentales del desarrollo

La investigación realizada por el Instituto Search ha identificado los siguientes elementos fundamentales del desarrollo como instrumentos para ayudar a los jóvenes a crecer sanos, interesados en el bienestar común y a ser responsables.

ELEMENTOS FUNDAMENTALES EXTERNOS

Apoyo

1. **Apoyo familiar**—La vida familiar brinda altos niveles de amor y apoyo.
2. **Comunicación familiar positiva**—El (La) joven y sus padres se comunican positivamente. Los jóvenes están dispuestos a buscar consejo y consuelo en sus padres.
3. **Otras relaciones con adultos**—Además de sus padres, los jóvenes reciben apoyo de tres o más personas adultas que no son sus parientes.
4. **Una comunidad comprometida**—El (La) joven experimenta el interés de sus vecinos por su bienestar.
5. **Un plantel educativo que se interesa por el (la) joven**—La escuela proporciona un ambiente que anima y se preocupa por la juventud.
6. **La participación de los padres en las actividades escolares**—Los padres participan activamente ayudando a los jóvenes a tener éxito en la escuela.

Fortalecimiento

7. **La comunidad valora a la juventud**—El (La) joven percibe que los adultos en la comunidad valoran a la juventud.
8. **La juventud como un recurso**—Se le brinda a los jóvenes la oportunidad de tomar un papel útil en la comunidad.
9. **Servicio a los demás**—La gente joven participa brindando servicios a su comunidad una hora o más a la semana.
10. **Seguridad**—Los jóvenes se sienten seguros en casa, en la escuela y en el vecindario.

Límites y expectativas

11. **Límites familiares**—La familia tiene reglas y consecuencias bien claras, además vigila las actividades de los jóvenes.
12. **Límites escolares**—En la escuela proporciona reglas y consecuencias bien claras.
13. **Límites vecinales**—Los vecinos asumen la responsabilidad de vigilar el comporamiento de los jóvenes.

14. **El comportamiento de los adultos como ejemplo**—Los padres y otros adultos tienen un comportamiento positivo y responsable.
15. **Compañeros como influencia positiva**—Los mejores amigos del (la) joven son un buen ejemplo de comportamiento responsable.
16. **Altas expectativas**—Ambos padres y maestros motivan a los jóvenes para que tengan éxito.

Uso constructivo del tiempo
17. **Actividades creativas**—Los jóvenes pasan tres horas o más a la semana en lecciones de música, teatro u otras artes.
18. **Programas juveniles**—Los jóvenes pasan tres horas o más a la semana practicando algún deporte, o en organizaciones en la escuela o de la comunidad.
19. **Comunidad religiosa**—Los jóvenes pasan una hora o más a la semana en actividades organizadas por alguna institución religiosa.
20. **Tiempo en casa**—Los jóvenes conviven con sus amigos "sin nada especial que hacer" dos o pocas noches por semana.

ELEMENTOS FUNDAMENTALES INTERNOS
Compromiso con el aprendizaje
21. **Motivación por sus logros**—El (La) joven es motivado(a) para que salga bien en la escuela.
22. **Compromiso con la escuela**—El (La) joven participa activamente con el aprendizaje.
23. **Tarea**—El (La) joven debe hacer su tarea escolar por lo menos durante una hora cada día de clases.
24. **Preocuparse por la escuela**—Al (A la) joven debe importarle su escuela.
25. **Leer por placer**—El (La) joven lee por placer tres horas o más por semana.

Valores positivos
26. **Preocuparse por los demás**—El (La) joven valora ayudar a los demás.
27. **Igualdad y justicia social**—Para el (la) joven tiene mucho valor el promover la igualdad y reducir el hambre y la pobreza.
28. **Integridad**—El (La) joven actúa con convicción y defiende sus creencias.
29. **Honestidad**—El (La) joven "dice la verdad aún cuando esto no sea fácil".
30. **Responsabilidad**—El (La) joven acepta y toma responsabilidad por su persona.
31. **Abstinencia**—El (La) joven cree que es importante no estar activo(a) sexualmente, ni usar alcohol u otras drogas.

Capacidad social
32. **Planeación y toma de decisiones**—El (La) joven sabe cómo planear y hacer elecciones.
33. **Capacidad interpersonal**—El (La) joven es sympático, sensible y hábil para hacer amistades.
34. **Capacidad cultural**—El (La) joven tiene conocimiento de y sabe convivir con gente de diferente marco cultural, racial o étnico.
35. **Habilidad de resistencia**—El (La) joven puede resistir la presión negativa de los compañeros así como las situaciones peligrosas.

36. **Solución pacífica de conflictos**—El (La) joven busca resolver los conflictos sin violencia.

Identidad positiva

37. **Poder personal**—El (La) joven siente que él o ella tiene el control de "las cosas que le suceden".
38. **Auto-estima**—El (La) joven afirma tener una alta auto-estima.
39. **Sentido de propósito**—El (La) joven afirma que "mi vida tiene un propósito".
40. **Visión positiva del futuro personal**—El (La) joven es optimista sobre su futuro mismo.

40 Acquis dont les jeunes ont besoin pour réussir

Le Search Institute a défini les pierres angulaires suivantes qui aident les jeunes à devenir des personnes saines, bienveillantes et responsables. Les pourcentages des jeunes détenant chaque acquis sont le fruit d'un sondage mené durant l'année scolaire 1999–2002 auprès de 220 100 jeunes Américains de la 6ᵉ à la 12ᵉ année.

ACQUIS EXTERNES
Soutien
1. **Soutien familial**—La vie familiale est caractérisée par un degré élevé d'amour et de soutien.
2. **Communication familiale positive**—Le jeune et ses parents communiquent positivement, et le jeune est disposé à leur demander conseil.
3. **Relations avec d'autres adultes**—Le jeune bénéficie de l'appui d'au moins trois adultes autres que ses parents.
4. **Voisinage bienveillant**—Le jeune a des voisins bienveillants.
5. **Milieu scolaire bienveillant**—L'école fournit au jeune un milieu bienveillant et encourageant.
6. **Engagement des parents dans les activités scolaires**—Les parents aident activement le jeune à réussir à l'école.

Prise en charge
7. **Valorisation des jeunes par la communauté**—Le jeune perçoit que les adultes dans la communauté accordent de l'importance aux jeunes.
8. **Rôle des jeunes en tant que ressources**—Le jeune se voit confier des rôles utiles dans la communauté.
9. **Service à son prochain**—Le jeune consacre à sa communauté au moins une heure par semaine.
10. **Sécurité**—Le jeune se sent en sécurité à la maison, à l'école et dans le quartier.

Limites et attentes
11. **Limites dans la famille**—La famille a des règlements clairs accompagnés de conséquences, et elle surveille les comportements du jeune.
12. **Limite à l'école**—L'école a des règlements clairs accompagnés de conséquences.
13. **Limites dans le quartier**—Les voisins assument la responsabilité de surveiller les comportements du jeune.

14. **Adultes servant de modèles**—Les parents et d'autres adultes dans l'entourage du jeune affichent un comportement positif et responsable.
15. **Influence positive des pairs**—Les meilleurs amis du jeune affichent un comportement responsable.
16. **Attentes élevées**—Les parents et les professeurs du jeune l'encouragent à réussir.

Utilisation constructive du temps
17. **Activités créatives**—Le jeune consacre au moins trois heures par semaine à suivre des cours de musique, de théâtre ou autres, et à mettre ses nouvelles connaissances en pratique.
18. **Programmes jeunesse**—Le jeune consacre au moins trois heures par semaine à des activités sportives, des clubs ou des associations à l'école et/ou dans la communauté.
19. **Communauté religieuse**—Le jeune consacre au moins trois heures par semaine à des activités dans une institution religieuse.
20. **Temps à la maison**—Le jeune sort avec des amis sans but particulier deux ou trois soirs par semaine.

ACQUIS INTERNES
Engagement envers l'apprentissage
21. **Encouragement à la réussite**—Le jeune est encouragé à réussir à l'école.
22. **Engagement à l'école**—Le jeune s'engage activement à apprendre.
23. **Devoirs**—Le jeune consacre au moins une heure par jour à ses devoirs.
24. **Appartenance à l'école**—Le jeune se préoccupe de son école.
25. **Plaisir de lire**—Le jeune lit pour son plaisir au moins trois heures par semaine.

Valeurs positives
26. **Bienveillance**—Le jeune estime qu'il est très important d'aider les autres.
27. **Égalité et justice sociale**—Le jeune accorde beaucoup d'attention à la promotion de l'égalité, et à la réduction de la faim et de la pauvreté.
28. **Intégrité**—Le jeune agit selon ses convictions et défend ses croyances.
29. **Honnêteté**—Le jeune « dit la vérité même si ce n'est pas facile ».
30. **Responsabilité**—Le jeune accepte et assume ses propres responsabilités.
31. **Abstinence**—Le jeune croit qu'il est important d'éviter d'être sexuellement actif et de consommer de l'alcool ou d'autres drogues.

Compétences sociales
32. **Planification et prise de décisions**—Le jeune sait comment planifier à l'avance et faire des choix.
33. **Aptitudes interpersonnelles**—Le jeune fait preuve d'empathie et de sensibilité, et noue des amitiés.
34. **Aptitudes culturelles**—Le jeune connaît des personnes d'autres cultures, races et ethnies, et se sent à l'aise avec elles.
35. **Résistance**—Le jeune est capable de résister à des pressions négatives exercées par ses pairs et à des situations dangereuses.
36. **Résolution pacifique de conflits**—Le jeune tente de résoudre les conflits sans recourir à la violence.

Identité positive

37. **Pouvoir personnel**—Le jeune sent qu'il a le contrôle sur les choses qui lui arrivent.

38. **Estime de soi**—Le jeune affirme avoir un degré élevé d'estime de soi.

39. **Sentiment d'utilité**—Le jeune croit que sa vie a un sens.

40. **Vision positive de l'avenir**—Le jeune est optimiste quant à son avenir personnel.

Assets You Need to Be a Peer Helper

Leader's Goals
1. To help students understand peer helping and its application to their daily lives
2. To increase students' knowledge of the 40 developmental assets and their importance for success
3. To discuss with the group how to show interest in another person in social situations
4. To help students initiate a conversation effectively
5. To help students handle nervousness in conversations

Students' Skill Development
1. Initiating a conversation effectively
2. Handling nervousness in conversations
3. Showing interest in another person in social situations

Leader's Tasks
1. To ask a volunteer to lead or co-lead the next session's homework review
2. To introduce activity: developing a list of what young people can do to build their own assets
3. To distribute observation assignments and explain this activity
4. To study the 40 assets and become very familiar with each of them

Materials Needed
1. A copy of the following for each group member:
   • Handout 4, Guidelines for Starting Conversations and the "W-H-E-A-T" conversation guide
   • Handout 5, The Power of Assets to Promote and Protect
2. Flip chart and easel
3. Observation assignments for each group member

Homework Review

1. What experiences did you have in getting to know the name or names of a classmate?
2. What did you learn about your classmates?
3. What did you learn about your parents and their names?

4. What other topics came up in your conversations with parents or guardians?
5. How did it feel to talk to parents about this subject?

When finished discussing the homework, tell the group you will be asking different members to lead the homework discussion for most sessions. The student leader will ask questions about the homework results and will choose the leader for the next session. You might suggest that someone volunteer to share the next session's leadership role with you. Let the volunteer know you will help her or him develop a list of questions if he or she would like.

SUMMARY OF THE PREVIOUS SESSION AND PURPOSE OF THIS SESSION

Start a practice of summarizing the previous session. Ask group members to share what they remember from that session and what had meaning for them. This helps build the connection between and relevance of the sessions.

Tell students that the purpose of this session is to help them gain a more thorough understanding of what they will be doing as peer helpers. They will learn how to start conversations, which is an essential skill for building relationships. Through the story of a girl named Mona, students will consider the qualities and skills needed to be a peer helper. They will also learn more about the 40 developmental assets.

UNDERSTANDING PEER HELPING

Because people have many different ideas about peer helping, it is important to discuss this concept so that group members gain a common understanding and a clearer focus of what they will be learning and doing. Ask group members what they think they will be doing once they have completed their training. After their sharing, ask questions such as these:
1. When you think of yourselves, friends, or classmates as a whole, what types of problems or issues do you see people having?
2. What kind of help do you think your peers often need?
3. How do peers hurt, rather than help, one another, making life even more difficult?
4. What kind of issues or problems might be inappropriate for a peer helper to deal with? Why?

Summarize the students' thoughts by clarifying misconceptions and stating what they will be learning and doing as peer helpers. Emphasize that the skills they acquire in these sessions will help them be effective in this new role. Give the group an easy definition—that peer helping is simply people helping people who are like them in some way—in this case, students helping students. Peer helpers are there for others who need someone to turn to for help, practical assistance, or support. Peer helpers encourage people when they experience frustrations, worries, concerns, or troublesome life events.

Name examples of formal peer helping such as peer tutoring, peer mediation, and peer counseling. Tell the students that peer helping can be as simple as listening while a friend describes a problem or more structured in format, such as educating others about substance abuse prevention.

INITIATING A SOCIAL RELATIONSHIP

The most basic skill peer helpers need is to be able to initiate social contact with others. To make friends, students need to know how to start conversations with others. People who are shy, lonely, or lack friendship skills often don't know how to begin or keep a conversation going. Some group members may fear being emotionally hurt or made fun of if they attempt to talk to someone they don't know outside the group. Some may fear not knowing what to say. Peer helpers need to know how to start conversations and establish a comfortable, trusting relationship with a person who needs a friend.

Learning Activity

Ask each member of the group to choose a partner, selecting someone he or she knows the least, and if possible, someone of the opposite sex. Having the students make the choice simulates what it feels like to initiate a conversation with someone you don't know. If there is an odd number, pick someone to be an observer, or offer yourself as a possible choice. **Do not leave anyone out.** Tell the group members you will give them 10 minutes to get acquainted with their partners. They can go anywhere in the room for their conversation.

Ten minutes may be hard for some, but this time period is significant. Some pairs may just wander around or sit in silence. Some may not even look at each other; however, don't intervene. All of your observations are subject matter for teaching this lesson.

If group members ask you how to begin, only tell them to start any way they choose. As a principle, tell them **what** to do, but not **how** to do it. The *how* provides the content for training development that the group needs. When 10 minutes are up, gather people back into a circle.

Processing the Activity

1. How did you feel when I asked you to choose someone you did not know?
2. How did you choose your partner?
3. If someone chose you, how did that make you feel?
4. How did you get started?
5. How many thought your partner was nervous? What made you think this?
6. How many thought you did most of the talking?

7. What effect did this have on your conversation?
8. What was it like to have silence in the conversation? How did you handle it?
9. What kinds of questions were you afraid to ask your partner? Why?
10. How easy is it for you to start a conversation with someone you don't know?
11. What difference does it make if the person is a different age or race than you?

REVIEWING GUIDELINES FOR STARTING CONVERSATIONS

Distribute Handout 4, Guidelines for Starting Conversations, and review it with the group. If you feel that your group needs more practice in initiating conversations, do the exercise again—this time with group members practicing some of the guideline suggestions.

REFLECTING ON MONA'S STORY

Before you read the story of Mona, ask each person to think of someone he or she knows whom students consider to be unintelligent, weird, or a loner. Group members will not identify this person to the group, but should think about why this person is viewed this way. After giving them a couple of minutes to reflect, read the story of Mona.

"How about her for the clumsiest girl? There must be a prize for that!"

I don't know who said it, but we all looked at the girl who was walking toward the lunch area.

"She isn't all that bad!" I offered.

"Well, Marcus, she sure won't be voted the most graceful girl in class," the first voice continued.

Someone else added, "Or even 299 out of 300!"

Mona—that was her name—couldn't have heard the remarks, but it was almost as if she had. Or maybe our thoughts showed on our faces. Anyway, just as she walked in front of us, Mona glanced our way and gave a shy smile. She had just murmured, "Hi," when her books began to slip. For one crazy second, she juggled her stuff in midair. Then everything fell—purse, books, papers—bounced and skittered all over the cement at our feet.

Somebody laughed. Mona's face turned red, and she dropped to her knees to gather up her belongings. Her fingers were trembling. I began to feel a little sorry for the poor kid and wished she'd hurry and get out of there. But when she was on her feet again, her face shiny with perspiration, her hair a mess, and her papers a jumble, a mocking voice stopped her as she turned to leave. It was Josh— athletic, popular Josh—who was known as the best-looking guy in school. "Hey," he shouted, "you missed one." And with his toe, in its big sneaker, he nudged a sheet of notebook paper that had floated under the table where he and a dozen other kids sat.

The paper had algebra problems figured neatly all over it. There was silence, I mean total silence, as we watched to see what Mona would do.

I think a few of us, me included, felt sort of ashamed by this time. But not enough to say, "Knock it off, Josh!" (As I said, Josh is popular. Very popular. Big, too!) Nobody offered to help, not even so much as to give the paper a shove, although 26 feet were planted right beside it. Then someone deliberately put a foot smack down on the paper. Mona hesitated, obviously wondering whether to forget the paper, turn, and run, or crawl in humiliation amid the legs of the guys and girls at the table to retrieve it. As we all sat wondering how she would get herself out of the miserable situation, a movement at a nearby table caught our attention.

Without saying a word, Alecia Ramirez slid off the bench, walked across the lunch area, got down on her knees, bent her gorgeous head, and crawled under the table. Everyone froze. We sat like statues. Mona's face was white by this time, and she looked sick, like she might cry at any moment. Josh's mouth hung open in a funny way, and a ring of gawking faces circled each table. Alecia (did I say she was gorgeous?), popular Alecia—always dressed great and looking terrific—hunched under the table surrounded by tennies of all sizes and shapes (and smelly, no doubt). Her hair fell across her brown eyes as she reached for that silly paper.

No one moved. No one blinked an eye as Alecia backed out, got to her feet, walked over, and tucked the paper into the jumble of stuff in Mona's arms. Mona mumbled "Thank you," and scurried away. Alecia walked back to her table, slid into place, picked up an apple, and took a bite. Crunch! It sounded like a volcano blowing its top.

That broke the spell. Suddenly lots of chatter and noise broke out, and with a lot of shoving and joking, we trooped back to class and the day went ahead as usual.

Before you discuss Mona's story, you may want to have students process their thoughts about the story in their journals. Then ask the following questions:

1. What do you think motivated Alecia to help Mona?
2. What may have kept Marcus from helping Mona?
3. What qualities and values did Alecia demonstrate by her actions?
4. How do people acquire these qualities and values?
5. What effect might Alecia's actions have had on the others who observed what she did?
6. What do you think you might have done if you had been there?
7. How much do you think physical appearance mattered in this scenario?

8. How does this story relate to what a peer helper might do or should do?

9. What might you do to reach out to the person you were thinking about before the reading of Mona's story?

10. Have you had experiences in which you could have reached out to help someone like Mona? What happened?

As members share the qualities and values Alecia demonstrated, write them on the flip chart for future reference.

INTRODUCING THE 40 DEVELOPMENTAL ASSETS

Ask group members to take out their list of the 40 assets with explanations of what each means and represents. Also distribute Handout 5, The Power of Assets to Promote and Protect. Explain how these items were identified, including the numbers of students surveyed to document them. Discuss the significance of the assets in terms of the students' personal growth and development and how these assets can affect their futures.

For example, you might say:

The list of developmental assets came from much reading, thinking, and discussion among researchers and people who work in communities for youth development. They asked the question, What do young people need to succeed? Once the list was made, researchers looked for and found hundreds of studies that supported these assets. They also created a survey to measure the numbers of assets young people have in their lives. Having surveyed more than 200,000 students in grades 6–12, researchers found that the more assets young people had, the better off they seemed to be. More assets mean more success and less trouble. For example, 8 percent of young people with 0–10 assets report that they get mostly A's on their report cards, compared to 47 percent of young people with 31–40 assets. And, 49 percent of young people with 0–10 assets report high alcohol use, compared to just 3 percent of young people with 31–40 assets. In simple language, these 40 assets are values, experiences, and qualities that young people need to be healthy, happy, responsible youth and adults.

After explaining the 40 assets, open a discussion about them.
1. Which assets seem the most important to you? Why?
2. Which ones don't you understand?
3. What surprises you about the 40 assets listed?
4. Do you feel some assets are not under your control to achieve? Why?
5. Which ones do you feel you most lack?
6. Which ones do you feel most of your peers lack?
7. Which ones did Alecia demonstrate in the Mona story?
8. Which assets apply to your work as peer helpers?
9. What do you feel you can do to help build your own assets?

Conclude the discussion by reminding the group that by building their own assets, they can become more effective peer helpers.

REFLECTING ON ASSETS

Draw students' attention back to the list of qualities and values that Alecia demonstrated in the story about Mona, and ask them which assets are highlighted there. Answers you can expect to hear include caring, integrity, interpersonal competence, positive peer influence, and self-esteem. Discuss with the group how having certain assets affects people's actions.

Ask group members which assets they are developing in learning to start conversations. The most likely answer you will hear is interpersonal competence. Begin a discussion on assets and relationships by asking, How will establishing a relationship with a new person help you build your assets?

Explain that as group members begin to share leadership roles (such as leading the homework review), they are developing the assets of responsibility and youth as resources.

HOMEWORK ASSIGNMENT

1. Ask group members to start a conversation with both a peer and an adult who is unfamiliar to them; however, caution them about approaching adults who are strangers. Suggest the students talk with a coworker of their parent or guardian, a teacher they don't know, a youth group leader, a store clerk, and so forth.
2. Ask students to start developing a list in their journals of what they can do to build assets for themselves.
3. Remind your student volunteer that he or she will lead or help lead the homework review at the next session.

Distribute Observation Assignments

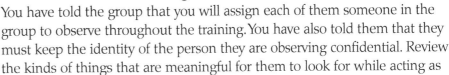

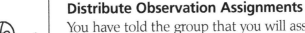

You have told the group that you will assign each of them someone in the group to observe throughout the training. You have also told them that they must keep the identity of the person they are observing confidential. Review the kinds of things that are meaningful for them to look for while acting as observers (pages 3–4). Tell the students that in Session 3 you will hand out some suggested guidelines for observations.

Distribute the slips indicating whom they should observe. **Be sure to keep a master list of your assignments for your own records.** Suggest that students make notes of their observations in their journals. Remind them that it is important to keep observations as positive as possible. However, they should **never** write down the name of the person they have been assigned. Tell the group that who observed whom will be revealed at the conclusion of the training.

1. Having a student lead the homework review encourages the group to do the homework, gives the leader a responsible role, and builds assets by contributing to her or his sense of positive identity.

2. If the Mona story does not seem appropriate for your particular group, find or write another story that is appropriate. The story should center on a youth demonstrating some aspect of peer helping that is relevant to the lives of those you are training.

3. The questions presented for processing discussions or activities are only suggestions. They are, however, questions that focus on what you are trying to teach or the points you are trying to make. Adapt them for your own use or develop your own questions, keeping in mind the focus of the discussion or activity.

4. It is vital that you be very familiar with the 40 assets and their connection to youth development. If you need more information, Search Institute in Minneapolis (www.search-institute.org) has a wealth of materials to help you grow in your knowledge of these assets. The more you know, the more you will be able to act as an asset builder for the students.

5. Give students the Search Institute Web site address. Students who enjoy surfing the Internet may like to find out more information about the 40 developmental assets this way. One important Search Institute resource you might consider giving each student is *Me@My Best: Ideas for Staying True to Yourself—Every Day,* which introduces young people to the eight categories of developmental assets.

6. You must prepare the observation assignments before this session. On a folded slip of paper for each person in the group, write the name of the **observer** on the outside of the slip and the **person to be observed** on the inside. Make sure that every person is both an **observer** and is being **observed.** Keep a list of who you have assigned to observe whom. Remind group members that, for the exercise to be helpful, it is critical that they not reveal the name of the person they are observing. Indicate that if Linda, for example, knows the identity of her observer, she may behave in ways that are not natural or usual—so confidentiality is key. This exercise can be powerful in many ways, as will be revealed when everyone shares her or his observations at the training's conclusion.

Guidelines for Starting Conversations

Ways to start conversations with someone you don't know:

1. Introduce yourself, if this is the first time you've spoken with the person.
2. Open the conversation with a topic that may be of interest to both of you. Ask a nonthreatening question. Comment on a piece of jewelry or clothing the other is wearing or a recent sports game. Or talk about something you both have in common.
3. Ask informational questions that can be used to continue the conversation or reveal a subject of interest to both. Example: "Where else have you lived?" "What classes do you enjoy the most?" "What youth events have you been to?"
4. Look at the person. Make eye contact and give the person your full attention.
5. Show you are listening by following a comment with an additional question or comment related to what the person has just said.
6. Return to the other person's comments about her- or himself without that person having to ask. Avoid an "interview" type of conversation by developing a "sharing" relationship.
7. As much as possible, avoid asking questions that can be answered with only a yes or a no. (See the W-H-E-A-T guide at the end of this handout.)
8. Smile occasionally, but try not to laugh or giggle unless appropriate. Not knowing you, the person may wonder if you are laughing at her or him.
9. Use questions and a tone of voice that convey sincerity and that are not mechanical.
10. Don't ask questions that deal with personal areas the person has not opened up about.
11. Allow for silences when the person may be considering how to answer or when you are both thinking of new directions in which to take the conversation.

W-H-E-A-T

The word *WHEAT* can be a handy, easy-to-remember guide for starting conversations. Each of the letters suggests a conversation topic:

Where you live: "Tell me about where you are from."
Hobby: "Tell me about your hobbies."
Event: "What was your experience like while you were at . . . ?"
Acquaintance: "How did you meet . . . ?"
Travel: "Tell me about your trip to . . . ."

The Power of Assets to Promote and Protect

Surveys of almost 150,000 students in grades 6–12 reveal that developmental assets are powerful influences on adolescent behavior. Assets both promote positive actions and attitudes and help protect young people from many different risky behaviors, regardless of students' gender, ethnic heritage, economic situation, or geographic location.

PROMOTING POSITIVE BEHAVIORS AND ATTITUDES

Search Institute research shows that the more assets students report having, the more likely they are to also report the following patterns of thriving behavior.

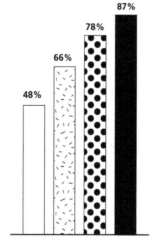

Exhibits Leadership
Has been a leader of an organization or group in the past 12 months.

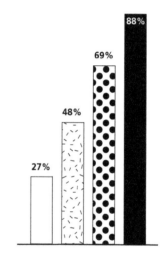

Maintains Good Health
Takes good care of body (such as eating foods that are healthy and exercising regularly).

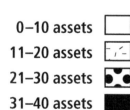

0–10 assets
11–20 assets
21–30 assets
31–40 assets

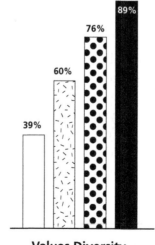

Values Diversity
Thinks it is important to get to know people of other racial/ethnic groups.

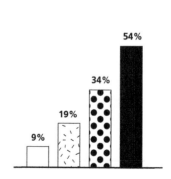

Succeeds in School
Gets mostly A's on report card (an admittedly high standard).

Session 2

PROTECTING YOUNG PEOPLE FROM HIGH-RISK BEHAVIOR

The more assets a young person reports having, the less likely he or she is to make harmful or unhealthy choices.

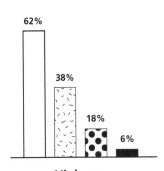

Violence
Has engaged in three or more acts of fighting, hitting, injuring a person, carrying a weapon, or threatening physical harm in the past 12 months.

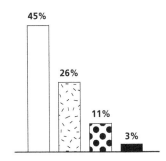

Problem Alcohol Use
Has used alcohol three or more times in the past 30 days or got drunk once or more in the past two weeks.

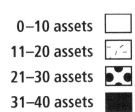

0–10 assets
11–20 assets
21–30 assets
31–40 assets

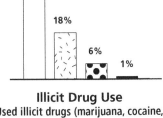

Illicit Drug Use
Used illicit drugs (marijuana, cocaine, LSD, PCP or angel dust, heroin, or amphetamines) three or more times in the past 12 months.

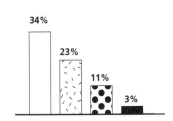

Sexual Activity
Has had sexual intercourse three or more times in lifetime.

Recognizing and Using the Assets You Have

Leader's Goals
1. To help students recognize how their lives have been shaped positively by the influence of others
2. To help students identify different ways people help others

Students' Skill Development
1. Learning trust through the sharing of personal experiences
2. Analyzing qualities and skills that affect the development of others
3. Participating in a leadership role

Leader's Tasks
1. To talk further about the observation assignments
2. To be prepared to talk about someone important in your life
3. To be prepared to share how someone has helped you in recent weeks

Materials Needed
1. List of questions your student leader can use for the homework discussion
2. A copy of Handout 6, Suggested Guidelines for Observations, for each group member
3. An index card (3 x 5 inches) for each group member
4. Flip chart and easel
5. Five pieces of poster board (may be cut in half), taped up around the room
6. At least five nontoxic markers in a variety of colors

Homework Review

Before the session begins, prepare the student who is to lead or co-lead the discussion on the homework by giving her or him some questions to use. However, urge the leader also to ask her or his own questions of interest. Explain that the purpose of the discussion is for group members to share their experiences of doing the homework, as well as to identify what they learned from completing the assignment. The following questions are examples:
1. What experiences did you have in starting conversations with strangers?

2. What was difficult about talking to an adult versus a peer? What was easy?
3. What reactions did you get from those to whom you talked?
4. What did you learn about the other person?

If some group members did not complete the homework, encourage them still to do so. Emphasize that the ability to talk with new people is such a basic skill for peer helping that it needs to be practiced. Some of the experiences of other group members may encourage the rest to try.

Have the student leader choose someone to take the responsibility of leading the homework discussion for the next session.

SUMMARY OF THE PREVIOUS SESSION AND PURPOSE OF THIS SESSION
Ask the group the following questions:
1. What do you remember from the last session?
2. What was most meaningful to you about that session?

Briefly describe what you will cover in this session: talking about someone important in your life and receiving help from others.

Observation Assignments
To help students learn what is useful to observe, distribute Handout 6, Suggested Guidelines for Observations, and review it as a group. Remind students what observations are and are not, as well as the kinds of behaviors for which they should be alert. Continue to stress confidentiality and keeping the observations as positive as possible.

TALKING ABOUT SOMEONE IMPORTANT IN YOUR LIFE
Ask each person to think of someone in her or his life who has had a significant positive influence on her or him. Some group members will probably want to say their parents or guardians have had such an influence. Because most people usually "expect" parents to help us in positive ways, encourage the students to consider someone who didn't "have" to take that kind of interest in them. Give students time to think. Then explain that you will go first. Share your story and then proceed around the circle. Group members don't have to say the person's name, but urge them to give details of how this person influenced them.

It is important that you as the leader go first for a number of reasons. By doing so, you demonstrate your willingness to share something personal. You also give the group ideas of the kinds of positive influences you want them to share. You model how to describe qualities about the person, as well as how to express feelings, which you want to encourage. For this sharing to be effective you must use a **true example from your life.** Here's the kind of story you might share:

My brother had a great influence on me when I was a teenager, a time when I was feeling very unattractive. He was six years older than me, good looking, and attending the local university. He took a great interest in me, sharing the books he was reading, attempting to teach me calculus, and inviting me to go with him to social functions that involved his classmates at the U. Whenever I was with him, he always acted proud of me. One time, though, when in a group of his friends, I was being quite silly. He didn't say anything then, but when we were alone, he told me how disappointed he was by my behavior, suggesting how he hoped I would act the next time. His interest in me helped me gain tremendous self-confidence and a willingness to accept some hard challenges so that I could grow.

Processing the Activity

Read each of the following questions and give students time to record some reflective responses in their journals. Then ask for volunteers to discuss their answers.

1. How did you feel about participating in this discussion?
2. What did you learn from sharing and listening to others?
3. What made this activity easy or difficult for you?
4. What did you learn from this activity about peer helping?
5. Who do you think would say that you have had a positive influence on her or him?
6. How could you pass on to others what you have been given by the person you described to the group?
7. How many of you have thanked the person for what he or she contributed to your life?

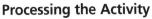

RECEIVING HELP FROM OTHERS

The group has been talking about relationships with a certain person whose influence occurred over a period of time. Focus next on specific acts of helpfulness that make a difference. Ask group members to think about experiences they have had more recently when someone helped them, made them feel better about themselves, or showed kindness to them. Share a personal example of what you are asking for; then give students time to think. Ask for five volunteers to participate in this activity while the rest observe.

First, point out the pieces of poster board and ask each of the volunteers to make a quick drawing or to write a few words representing the experience he or she will talk about. Then, place the volunteers in the center, as the others gather around them in a circle. Give the five volunteers three minutes each (15 minutes total) to share their experiences and reflect on different ways people have helped them. Then ask the observing group to point out additional ways of helping they heard that weren't mentioned specifically. List all the ways mentioned on the flip chart.

Processing the Activity

1. How did those of you in the inner group feel about sharing?
2. What did those of you observing learn from listening?

3. What do you see as the relationship between your experiences and peer helping?
4. What have you done in the past week or months to help others?

REFLECTING ON ASSETS

Talk about the asset of adult role models and how the important people in their lives have helped the group members to build assets. Ask group members to state the qualities, actions, or characteristics that were identified as each student spoke earlier about the important person in her or his life. Write these qualities, actions, and characteristics on the flip chart for all to see. When the group is finished, review the list. Ask how these important qualities, actions, and characteristics fit with the developmental assets.

Have group members take out their list of 40 assets and identify the assets that were mentioned in the students' sharing. Write these on the flip chart. Direct the students' attention to the breakdown into external and internal assets. Explain that external assets usually require people in the environment to help a young person experience them. Internal assets are ones young people can more easily develop for themselves.

Ask students to think about which assets they now feel they have. Then ask group members to choose the ones they think they need to work on for themselves. Finally, have each member choose both an external and an internal asset he or she wants to develop or strengthen during the training. Start the sharing process by telling the ones you want to work on for yourself as a leader. Have the students write their goals on index cards for you to collect (ask them to sign the card).

This is a good time to remind group members that they all can act as peer helpers by working with one another to build the two assets each has declared. Also, seeing people work to attain these goals can become part of their observation assignment. Tell the group that for the next session you will prepare and distribute a list with each member's goals as a reminder of everyone's commitment and willingness to help one another.

What Students Can Do to Build Assets for Themselves

Ask the group members to turn to the lists they began in their journals of what they can do to build their own assets (starting this list was part of the homework assignment for Session 2). Have them compare the actions just shared with the ideas on their lists. Have them add the actions mentioned if they are not already on their lists. Have the students share the other ideas they have on their lists. Encourage them to continue to think of creative ways in which they can build assets for themselves.

HOMEWORK ASSIGNMENT

1. Suggest that, if possible, students write a thank-you to the person they talked about in the circle. Expressing appreciation shows caring and can help strengthen a relationship.

2. Have group members ask a parent or other adult about someone who has been a positive influence in her or his life, and how that person has affected her or him.

3. Have each person come prepared to share an achievement of which he or she is proud. It does not have to be a major event. It could be something as simple as getting out of bed in the morning to go to school or teaching something to a younger brother or sister. The students will talk about these accomplishments with a partner at the next session.

Notes for Leaders

1. The purpose of talking about someone important is to help group members realize the assets they have experienced through people who were under no obligation to take an interest in them but were motivated to do so. This is the basic premise of peer helping—building relationships and doing something for others just because you care. If members of your group cannot think of anyone except their parents who has influenced them in a positive way, then invite them to share what their parents have done.

2. If members of the group think there is no one in their life who has had a positive influence, ask them to talk about the kind of help they would like to receive, as well as the kind of person they would like to have in their life. If someone is unwilling or unable to do this, don't push. You want this to be a good experience for your group and certainly don't want anyone to feel worse about her- or himself. If you sense that anyone has been bothered by this activity, ask to speak to her or him later privately.

3. Highlighting the list of qualities, actions, and characteristics represented by group members' stories of people in their lives makes students aware of the personal influence they can have on others, particularly after they learn the skills being taught.

4. The list of qualities generated during discussion helps students understand the 40 assets. Take plenty of time to have them study the list. Compare the group's list to the 40 developmental assets, particularly with respect to the support assets. This will help students understand more concretely the power and importance of the assets.

5. Having students publicly declare which assets they want to work on increases their commitment to building these assets and motivates group members to help each other reach their goals. While observing one another, they become more alert to changes in the direction of achieving these personal goals.

6. Another activity you might want to include in the Reflecting on Assets section involves use of the set of eight *In Our Own Words* posters from Search Institute that cover each of the asset categories. You could put these up around the room and have students get into groups by category. Then, using the quotes on the posters from young people as inspiration, individuals in your group can come up with their own words and phrases to describe the assets in their category.

Suggested Guidelines for Observations

BEHAVIORS

- How does the person generally relate to others in the group?
- What are the usual expressions on the person's face and how do these affect others?
- Which of the person's behaviors contribute to the benefit of the group?
- Which behaviors distract the group or cause problems?
- What positive changes in the person's behavior have you observed?
- What is the person's general pattern of participation in the group in terms of attendance and homework assignments?
- Does the person tend to be a leader or a follower? How so?

ATTITUDES

- How does the person usually respond to what is going on in the group?
- How does the person deal with ideas different from her or his own?
- How much does the person trust the group? How openly does he or she share?
- How much is the person willing to risk or try in order to learn new skills?
- What are the person's usual reactions to the lessons and homework in terms of importance?

ASSETS

- What assets do you observe this person as having or building as you watch her or him in this group?
- How has this person helped others in the group build assets?

The Mission of Peer Helping

Leader's Goals
1. To encourage students to share an achievement
2. To have students self-reflect on personal skills and qualities as well as assets
3. To encourage student contributions for a peer helping mission statement

Students' Skill Development
1. Sharing an achievement
2. Identifying skills and qualities represented by this achievement
3. Developing a mission statement

Leader's Tasks
1. To distribute list of group member names with individual asset goals
2. To describe the thought card activity and its purpose
3. To share a true personal achievement
4. To introduce the writing of a peer-helping mission statement

Materials Needed
1. Flip chart and easel
2. A copy of the Le Guin quote on page 38 for each group member
3. Copies of sample mission statements
4. Index cards or copies of Handout 7 for the thought card activity

Homework Review

Call on the person chosen to lead this discussion. Always check with the student leader before the session to see if he or she is ready or needs help. Examples of questions to cover in the sharing include the following (however, urge the student leader to ask her or his own questions of interest):
1. What was the reaction when you connected with the important person in your life?
2. Was the contact made by phone, letter, email, or in person?
3. What did you learn from asking your parent or another adult about an important person in her or his life?
4. What surprised you about these conversations?
5. What did you learn from this experience?

Have the student leader choose someone to take the responsibility of guiding the homework discussion for the next session.

The focus of the homework review is having group members relate feelings and what they have learned. Discussing the homework emphasizes its importance and encourages others to try it. Talking to parents or other adults becomes easier when it is an "assignment," and it is hoped that the homework will open a new channel of communication between students and their parent(s).

SUMMARY OF THE PREVIOUS SESSION AND PURPOSE OF THIS SESSION

Give each group member the list of the group's individual asset goals. Have students review the goals they have chosen. Ask if any of them would like to change their goals. If any students would like to make alterations, ask them to state their new goal and have all students write the update on their papers. Remind group members to keep track in their journals of their own progress toward their goals and to record the progress of the person they have been assigned to observe. When students are done making changes, ask the following questions:

1. What was the most important thing you remember from the preceding session?
2. How has this made a difference in your peer relationships? in your family relationships?
3. What have you done that you didn't "have" to do to help someone since the last session?
4. What was least helpful about the preceding session?

Use your own words to summarize the purpose of this session for students.

During the training, you invite members of your group to write their own peer-helping mission statement—a daunting task for almost anyone. Writing a peer-helping mission statement provides practice in conceptualizing a mission statement and encourages ownership and application of what they are learning.

Some young people may not understand the full significance of a mission, but they can be led to think of their gifts and the use of their gifts for and with others. The achievement activity helps uncover some of the individual gifts each person has.

SHARING ACHIEVEMENTS

Explain that often when we accomplish something, we overlook the talents that we used to gain our achievement. Someone listening may more objectively identify these overlooked skills. This careful listening is "mining" a person's skills and qualities from a story being told.

Demonstrate this activity by asking a volunteer to listen to you share a fairly simple achievement. An example might be as follows:

When I was in high school, I realized that our town needed a teen center for young people to hang out. I was a member of the student council, and so I brought up the idea. The council agreed it was a good idea but didn't know how to go about starting one. I decided to approach a favorite teacher, who I thought would understand. She was willing to help me, and together we drew up a list of what would have to be done. The first step was finding a possible location. I brainstormed with the council as to possible sites, and one was the YWCA. Another council member and I approached the Y. We presented our proposal, indicating that we would cover all costs to make a space ready, and we assured the Y staff that our activities would not cause any damage or problems. We did not get an immediate answer; the staff had questions about sponsorship, how the space would be used, and insurance.

I returned to my teacher for help. She suggested approaching the parent-teacher organization for sponsorship, including some financial investment into the project. I went to the principal and the city council with a request for money. After much discussion and persuasion, with the help of others on the student council, we got permission to use a basement room of the YWCA with an outside exit. It needed painting and a few repairs, but we organized school volunteers to take care of these things, and eventually the space was ready. We promoted the center by writing articles in the school newspaper and passing out flyers. I even wrote an article for the local newspaper.

I appointed various classmates to be in charge of different aspects of the opening: food, ticket taking, chaperoning, music, and entertainment. Finally, opening night arrived, and kids were waiting at the door. They poured in, and the huge crowd spent the evening dancing and playing games until we closed at midnight. We had done it—our center was launched.

Make two columns on the flip chart, heading one **Skills** and the other **Qualities.** Ask your listener to identify skills and qualities this description represented, and as he or she does so, list them under the appropriate headings. Examples might be organizational skills and quality of perseverance. When the volunteer has finished, you and the rest of the group should add any that you thought were missed.

Before assigning them to pairs, be sure the students understand what they are to do. Remind them that coming prepared to talk about a personal achievement was part of the homework assignment in the preceding session. One person will describe an achievement, while the listener writes down or remembers the person's skills or qualities demonstrated. The listener then shares what he or she heard. Then the roles are reversed. Allow sufficient time, as valuable conversations might emerge in the pairs.

Afterward, process the activity by asking questions such as the following:

1. What did you learn about yourself by doing this activity?
2. What surprised you about what your listener heard?
3. What made it hard to identify the qualities or skills from the story told?
4. What skills and qualities did the speaker recognize in her- or himself by sharing?
5. Which of these skills and qualities would be useful for a peer helper?

When the discussion is finished, ask group members to record in their journals the skills and qualities that their partners identified.

THE THOUGHT CARD

Introduce the thought card activity to be done for each session hereafter. The ongoing thought card stimulates deep reflection among the group members about themselves and what is important in their lives. In the process each person writes her or his name and a thought on a card or paper (see Handout 7 for thought cards you can copy and cut out for students). You may want to offer students an email option rather than exchanging cards. Students who have their own email accounts and access to computers may communicate more openly this way.

The students' thought could be about anything important to them related to peer helping—their relationships with others, desires, concerns, or their own development of specific assets. Group members turn the cards in to you each session. You provide them with a response that may lead them to better understand or pursue deeper feelings or life-shaping ideas. The purpose of your response is not to give advice, but rather to reflect back constructively. Emphasize that no one else in the group will know of these thoughts and responses—they will be kept confidential.

To help students understand what you want them to do, distribute the following quote from Ursula K. Le Guin's *Very Far Away from Anywhere Else* and read it aloud:

I think what you mostly do when you find you really are alone is to panic. You rush to the opposite extreme and pack yourself into groups . . . clubs, teams, societies, types. You suddenly start dressing exactly like the others. It's a way of being invisible. The way you sew the patches on the holes in your blue jeans becomes incredibly important. If you do it wrong you're not with it. You have to be with it. That's a peculiar phrase, you know? With it. With what? With them. With the others. All together. Safety in numbers. I'm not me. I'm a basketball letter, I'm a popular kid. I'm my friend's friend. I'm a black leather growth on a Honda. I'm a member. I'm a teenager. You can't see me, all you can see is us. We're safe.

Then have the students pair up and read it together, asking them to think about their feelings and reactions to what Owen, a senior in high school, is saying. Read the quote aloud again and discuss the group's thoughts and reactions.

As the group discusses this passage, pay particular attention to feelings expressed and note them for future use when teaching about feelings vocabularies in Session 7. Ask:
1. What thoughts or feelings did this passage bring to mind?
2. Compared to your experience, what feels real about Owen's statement?
3. When have you felt alone and panicked?
4. How did you handle this feeling of being alone?
5. Is there a price to pay if you choose not to become part of a group? Explain.
6. What are clues that someone isn't part of a group in your school?
7. How much does a group define how you feel about yourselves?
8. What could you do to reach out to someone who you think feels alone?

PEER-HELPING MISSION STATEMENT

Now, to help them gain focus and understanding of what they are learning and why, have group members integrate what they have learned into a peer-helping mission statement.

Introduce this project by explaining that every organization, magazine, and social service agency has a mission statement that guides and directs its work. It would be useful for them to write a similar statement for the work they want to do.

Read or distribute samples of mission statements to give group members an idea of what you mean. Here are some examples:

"To build a world in which youth and adults learn, grow, and work together as catalysts for positive change." (4-H)

"To make a positive difference in the lives of children and youth." (Big Brothers Big Sisters of America)

"To inspire and enable all young people . . . to realize their full potential as productive, responsible, caring citizens." (Boys and Girls Clubs of America)

Have the group members talk about what is meaningful for them in these statements. Which missions seem more important or real? Then have group members identify words or ideas that convey what peer helping means to them. Questions to help students build a list of words include: Who is the target group for their work? How will group members know if they are accomplishing their mission?

When they seem to have exhausted their ideas, divide students into groups of three and ask them to draft a mission statement that fits their understanding of what they will be trying to do as peer helpers, whom they will be serving, and the settings in which peer helping will take place. Explain that this initial attempt does not need to be perfect because after they hand in their drafts, you will synthesize their ideas and present the resulting statement to the group at the next session.

REFLECTING ON ASSETS

Ask students to look at the list of skills and qualities that their partner identified in the "mining" activity. Have them look at the 40 developmental assets. How many of their identified skills and qualities fit in with or relate to the assets? For example, having organizational skills could demonstrate that they are good at planning and decision making, whereas being persistent may demonstrate taking responsibility and having a sense of purpose. Have students share some of the assets they demonstrated in their achievement. At the end of the discussion give students some time to write down in their journals the assets they demonstrated in their achievement.

HOMEWORK ASSIGNMENT

1. Have the students talk to an adult family member or another adult to whom they feel close about the students' achievements and what they learned about themselves. Then have students ask the adult to tell them about one of her or his own achievements. Have group members practice identifying skills and qualities by giving feedback to the adult about which of these they recognized in her or his story.

2. Ask group members to make a stick figure drawing of themselves at the center of a page in their journals. Tell them to surround the drawing with words and phrases that identify their skills and qualities.

3. Remind students to continue adding ideas in their journal of what they can to do to build their own assets. Perhaps new ideas were triggered by this session.

1. Although a true example of a person's achievement is provided, using a true achievement from your own life is more effective and authentic. Try to include as many different examples of skills and qualities that this achievement demonstrated, but keep your story clear and simple.

2. Emphasize confidentiality when explaining the thought card activity and remind students not to worry about spelling or grammar; you are only interested in the content of the thought.

3. When responding to their thoughts, try to point out links or themes to peer-helping work. Emphasize the positive and look for feelings expressed.

4. Whenever you are dividing the group for various activities, try to mix or pair different people together. A frequent method is to number off, and then group together based on the numbers. For example, if you have nine in your group and you want three groups of three, have students count off to three, then three again, and then a third time. When done, ask the 1s to get together, the 2s, and so on.

5. If your program is taking place in a school or youth organization, include your school or youth organization's mission statement among the examples given here.

6. You don't need to achieve a polished mission statement. The purpose is to gather group members' thoughts and understandings about peer helping and to inspire their ongoing commitment to this work. Take what students develop in the small groups and synthesize the main ideas into several possible statements, using as many student ideas as possible. Share these mission statement drafts with them at the next session, seeking their reactions and choices.

7. Remember to act in asset-building ways when you are engaging with the students. Refer to the sidebar on pages xiv–xv in the introduction for ideas on how to be a good role model for group members.

Thought Cards

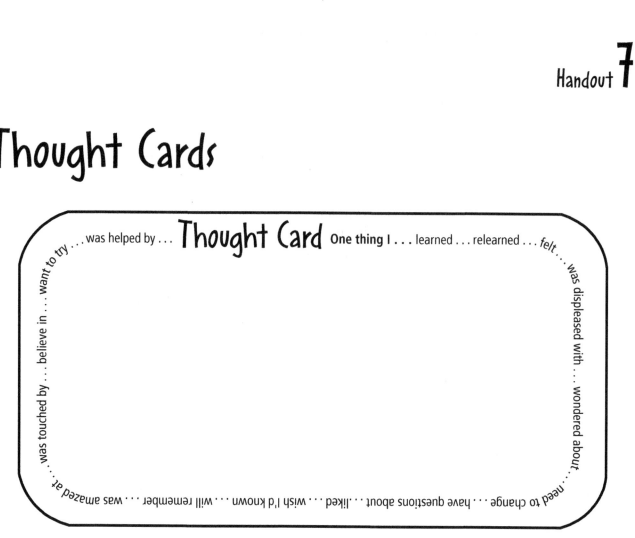

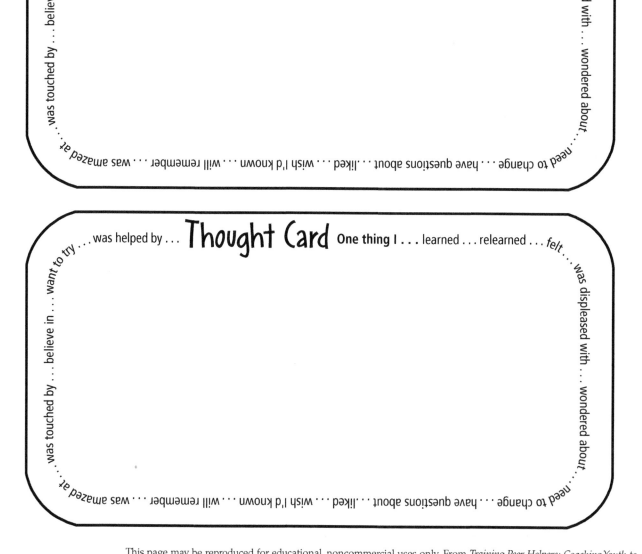

Communication Skills: Asking Questions

Leader's Goals

1. To help the group identify and use four types of conversational questions: Closed, Open, Informational, and Personal
2. To demonstrate the power of using open-ended questions to establish meaningful interpersonal relationships
3. To introduce the group to a variety of personal interests

Students' Skill Development

1. Identifying and using the four types of questions for different conversational purposes
2. Helping another person share her or his interests, when the interest is new to the questioner
3. Establishing a conversational bridge with someone students want to know or help by using open-ended questions

Leader's Tasks

1. To distribute synthesis of peer-helping mission statements
2. To distribute blank thought cards
3. To collect thought cards for your response

Materials Needed

1. Flip chart and easel
2. A copy of Handout 8, Guidelines for Using Questions in Conversations, for each group member
3. Cards for thought card activity

Homework Review

Call on your student leader to guide students in discussing what happened when they talked to parents or adults about past achievements. Highlight skills or qualities revealed in these conversations that were not mentioned during the previous session. Encourage students to share some of the words they wrote to describe their skills and qualities.

Have the student leader pick someone to conduct the next session's homework review.

SUMMARY OF THE PREVIOUS SESSION AND PURPOSE OF THIS SESSION

Ask group members what was most and least meaningful to them about the preceding session. Was there anything they didn't understand?

Distribute your synthesis of the students' small-group mission statements and discuss their reactions. Which statement best fits the group? What, if anything, is missing? If there are concerns, ask for volunteers to continue working on a statement to bring to the next session.

Collect group members' thought cards and distribute cards to share thoughts for the next session. From time to time, you might want to give group members a particular focus for the thought card, especially if difficult issues arise.

In your own words summarize the following material to give students an idea of what they will be learning in this session.

Most people ask hundreds of questions each week as the main tool for verbal interaction with others. Yet few people are skilled in asking the kinds of questions that draw people closer and deepen self-understanding, or the kinds of questions that lead others to the answers they seek about life and their problems. Professional interviewers, such as Barbara Walters and Katie Couric, are paid handsomely for their questioning skills. They ask the questions we want to ask or may not think to ask, and they assist those interviewed to share their feelings, thoughts, and values with others.

Questioning is an important skill to learn, especially because the peers that group members will be asked to help may lack social skills. Learning how to ask different types of questions helps establish sincere, warm, and helpful relationships. Peer helpers need to know how to ask the questions that build relationships, encourage others, affirm a person's value, and allow the sharing of significant feelings.

Many of us fear reaching out to someone we don't know because we don't know how to *establish a bridge* for conversation. Appropriate questions can build this bridge.

Emphasize in this session that you are not suggesting that group members go around interviewing everyone—questions are only part of the conversation process. Listening and sharing are also important, as is sincerity in wanting to know the person with whom they are talking. Every person deserves a listener's respect, interest, and concern.

This lesson focuses on the use of open-ended and personal questions, but point out that we frequently have to start conversations by asking for information. If we asked only open-ended questions, people would probably avoid us because we would not function effectively. The demonstration activity illustrates the need we sometimes have to gather basic information as a foundation for beginning a more in-depth conversation.

DEMONSTRATING FOUR TYPES OF QUESTIONS

1. Tell group members to think about two of their most unusual interests that are important to them. These interests should be ones that they turn to for relaxation, discovery, and/or fun. The students don't have to know a great deal about these interests. They may be interests that most people would not suspect the students have. However, they should be genuine interests. Going around the circle, group members will state their two interests but will not talk about or explain them. If the interest is so unique that most group members would not understand what it is, the person can give a brief explanation. **Give the group time to think before you start the sharing.**

2. **Do not go first this time as the leader.** Doing so might influence the students' choice of interests. Instead, ask for a volunteer to start and share when your turn comes in the circle.

3. After all have named two interests, pick the person with the most unusual interest or a person you want to draw into the group's interaction. Ask this person if he or she would be willing to have the group ask questions about the selected interest. Choosing the most unusual interest will allow you to demonstrate that even if we don't know anything about another person's interests, with skillful and appropriate questioning, we can establish a meaningful conversation.

4. Ask the group to brainstorm questions to ask the focus person about this interest. Indicate that you do not expect the person to answer the questions at this time. As students ask questions, write them on the flip chart, verbatim. This is critical to what you are teaching. When you have several questions, continue with the next step.

5. Turn to the focus person and explain that although he or she might like to answer all the questions on the chart, you would like her or him to indicate only those that would be particularly satisfying to answer—in other words, questions that would be fun to answer, not ones the focus person thinks the group wants a response to, nor the ones whose answers might impress the group.

6. Read aloud the questions on the chart and mark those the person would like to answer. Ask students what differences they see between questions the person would like to answer and those not chosen. Often, but not always, people select the **open-ended and/or personal questions,** which allow the person to share something about her- or himself, such as an achievement or unusual knowledge, without sounding as if he or she were bragging.

7. Have the person answer one marked question for the group. Ask group members what other questions they might ask now, based on the person's answer. These new questions show that answers can give "free" information, often related to another topic, which can be used to go further with a conversation.

8. Explain to the group that essentially there are only four types of

questions people ask: **Closed, Open-ended, Informational,** and **Personal.** Make a chart everyone can see illustrating these four types.

	Personal	**Informational**
Closed	Do you get scared doing it?	Does it cost much money?
Open-ended	What unusual experiences have you had doing this?	What kinds of caves have you explored?

The chart gives examples of closed personal and closed informational questions. Closed questions require us either to ask another question or discontinue the conversation because they tend to elicit one-word or one-sentence responses. Open-ended personal and open-ended informational questions open the door to much more content and can be used to move the conversation forward. Frequently, they hint at what the person wants to talk about. Many of us are nervous about conversations with strangers because we worry about running out of questions; open-ended questions help keep a conversation going.

9. We may sometimes be afraid to ask personal or open-ended questions because we think we are prying into another person's life. People often are eager, however, to have someone show that kind of interest in them because it gives them a chance to share what's important to them. This kind of sharing builds relationships.

10. Most open-ended questions begin with *What, Where, When,* or *How.* Questions with these words anticipate an answer of more than just one word or statement. *Why* questions also are open-ended, but must be used carefully, because often people cannot answer them easily and might feel put on the defensive. Sometimes we just don't know why we do what we do or feel what we feel. Soften *why* questions by asking, "I *wonder* why you feel . . . ?" This gives the person an opportunity to say something like, "I'm not sure myself." Rudyard Kipling once said, "I keep six honest men serving me. They taught me all I know: Their names are What and Why and When and How and Where and Who." This is good advice to put into our conversational tool kit.

11. Go through the list on the chart and ask the group to identify each question by type. Ask how students might turn a closed question into an open one. Example: "Do you get scared doing it?" can be changed to "What about this can be scary?" or "What can be difficult about this hobby for you?" The person might respond that nothing is scary or might give additional information about the activity's difficulty or thrill.

The demonstration illustrates that people prefer to answer open-ended or personal questions more than closed or informational ones. However, most people are programmed to ask safe, closed informational questions that can be answered specifically. Open-ended and personal questions (those that ask about feelings and values) invite the other person to share about her- or himself and allow the person to safely reveal events and emotions, which may lead to a closer relationship. Likewise, effective open-ended questions can help a person gain new self-understanding because they lead her or him to think about something in a new way.

When asked an open-ended question, a person usually shares important information that is "tucked into" the specific question's answer. Picking up on this "free" information not only shows that you are listening but also takes the conversation to a deeper level. Sometimes this moves the conversation to a different topic—one with greater meaning for the individual you are talking to.

PRACTICING QUESTIONING SKILLS

1. Divide students into groups of three. Always make yourself available if needed to ensure the right number for the activity.
2. Each small group's task is to interview one another about one of the interests shared in the demonstration. The person whose interest you focused on earlier in the demonstration should choose another interest or act as the observer of the entire group. One member of the group starts questioning the other. The task is to practice questioning the other person about the interest, particularly trying to use open-ended questions. So the questioner should not respond as he or she normally would in a conversation, but the partner *should* answer the questions posed unless he or she chooses not to. The third person acts as a "referee" to stop the person being questioned from giving away "free information" when asked a closed-ended question. The referee can also help the interviewer come up with questions if he or she gets stuck. After five minutes the group members switch roles: the first interviewer becomes the one being questioned, the referee becomes the interviewer, and the one being questioned becomes the referee. Shift one more time so that each member of the small groups has a chance to take on each role.
3. **Be sure to instruct those being questioned to answer closed questions with closed answers.** Students should not elaborate if asked a closed question. When all members have had a chance at all three roles, call the group back together to process the activity.

Processing the Activity

1. What was hard about this activity?
2. What did you learn about yourself during this activity?
3. What did you learn about the use of open-ended questions?
4. How did you use answers to help you ask further questions?
5. What other topics besides the initial interest emerged from the questioning?
6. How much did you learn about your partners versus the subject of interest?

7. How many of you found you only had to ask one or two questions to gain a lot of information from your partners? How did this happen?
8. What questions were not asked about your interest that you wished your partners had asked?
9. What might make it hard to ask a person questions about a subject of similar interest?
10. How did a question help you get to know yourself better?
11. What kind of feelings did this activity evoke?
12. How often do you experience people asking open-ended questions about you?
13. What kind of questions do you ask family members?
14. What kind of questions do members of your family ask you?

Guidelines for Using Questions in Conversations

When doing this activity, students often don't know how to start the questioning, especially when trying to practice open-ended questioning. Distribute Handout 8, Guidelines for Using Questions in Conversations, and review it with the group. Then arrange the students in groups of three again, this time using new partners. Each group observer should watch for differences that occur between this practice and the previous one.

After the students have finished, explain that questions such as those in the guidelines tend to deepen a relationship by exploring self-reflection, showing genuine respect, and extending the horizons of what we know about ourselves and others.

REFLECTING ON ASSETS

Ask students to think about the assets they have built or strengthened through the skills learned in this session. The purpose of the thought card activity is to develop deeper self-reflection, leading to greater personal power, sense of purpose, and positive view of personal future—all positive-identity assets. Learning to ask questions improves interpersonal competence and can help build the assets of cultural competence, honesty, caring, and positive peer influence. Other assets students might mention include youth as resources, other adult relationships, adult role models, and creative activities. After the discussion, ask students to record in their journals the assets they feel they have personally strengthened through this session.

HOMEWORK ASSIGNMENT

1. Have the students interview an adult outside their family about an interest he or she has. Adults usually enjoy talking about their interests and may be flattered that a young person would ask. To make the experience appealing, the students should try to find someone who has an interest or hobby that they know little about.
2. Ask students to bring in their thought cards or email you.
3. Explain that during the next session they will meet a "secret visitor" with whom they can practice their questioning skills.

1. If the students agree with most of the mission statement, adopt it. If not, ask for some volunteers to work on it on their own time. The important point is for the students to write the statement, not you. When a final draft has been approved, post it for review at each session. You might get mission statement cards made for students to carry or print out copies of the mission statement on large, peel-off labels to affix to the cover of their journals.

2. Questions not asked that students wish had been asked furnish an important discussion topic. Often, when we talk to someone else, we ask questions to satisfy our own curiosity, rather than exploring what the other person wants to tell us. The subject may not interest us, but hopefully we are interested in the person. Centering attention on our conversation partner conveys respect and affirms her or his self-worth.

3. The previous point also holds true when talking to someone who shares a similar interest. Often, we may not ask a question because we think we know the answer. However, we don't know the answer through the other person's experiences and opinions. A basic principle always to remember is that we are not researching a subject; we are trying to get to know a person.

4. Sometimes a person acknowledges learning something about her- or himself from a question. Highlight this possibility, emphasizing that someone else's thoughtful question can be a powerful tool in building a relationship, even in a brief, but sincere, conversation. Responses to the question of how frequently the students are asked open-ended questions can also emphasize the power of questions in building relationships. People are hungry to have someone think enough about a social exchange to ask them thoughtful open-ended questions.

5. Be sure to emphasize how frequently we ask closed questions. We don't have to be taught how to ask questions such as, Can I? Will you? Are you? We also don't realize how programmed we are to do this because adults often elaborate when asked such questions. However, shy or insecure young people (or adults) most likely won't do the same. Peers often avoid approaching them because they are not skilled in social interaction. Peer helpers should reach out to such people.

6. To reinforce the importance of asking open-ended questions, notice that most of the questions in this training, particularly in the process work, are stated as open-ended questions.

Guidelines for Using Questions in Conversations

▲ To start a conversation, you usually have to ask a few closed informational questions such as: Where are you from? What grade are you in? Do you have any brothers or sisters? What are some of your interests? Usually the answers to such questions give enough information to explore more personal topics.

▲ You "try out" different subjects during the first part of a conversation with a new person because you're trying to discover what topic that person feels comfortable discussing. Clues to what an individual might want to talk about include how he or she emphasizes a particular response and when he or she gives more information.

▲ Saying "Tell me something about yourself" to draw out another person doesn't work well; it sounds mechanical to a new acquaintance and requires the other person to do the work. He or she must guess what might interest you, and that can be un-nerving. Asking what kinds of interests the person has provides a focus for her or his reply.

▲ Acknowledge when your new friend names an interest or topic that is totally foreign to you. Then follow with, "Would you tell me something about . . . ?" Listen for details in the explanation to give you clues about what to ask next.

▲ You then can ask additional open-ended questions such as:
How did you get involved in this interest?
What makes this interest special to you?
What is the most fascinating thing that has happened to you related to this interest?
What have you learned from pursuing this interest?

If the topic is something other than a personal interest, you can ask specific questions such as:
What is it about this subject that frustrates you?
What do you feel are the differences between our two cultures?
What affected you the most about the book you were reading?
What are some of the things you look forward to after you graduate?

Communication Skills: Listening

Leader's Goals
1. To demonstrate the appropriate use of questioning
2. To help students recognize biases (filters) that affect listening

Students' Skill Development
1. Applying the skill of questioning to learn about a new person
2. Learning the difference between listening and hearing

Leader's Tasks
1. To return thought cards with your comments, collect thought cards for your response, and distribute blank thought cards
2. To arrange for a "secret visitor" to meet your group. This can be the school principal, city mayor, a pastor, an elder, a rabbi, a priest, or a businessperson. It should be someone the group doesn't know well and perhaps someone you would like to familiarize with your program.

Materials Needed
1. Flip chart and easel
2. Cards for thought card activity

Homework Review

Ask the student leader to begin the homework discussion. Highlight the variety of interests that were revealed by the interviews with adults. Encourage group members to share some of what they learned about these various interests and to describe how the conversations sparked any curiosity in learning more.

SUMMARY OF THE PREVIOUS SESSION AND PURPOSE OF THIS SESSION

1. How have you tried to use open-ended questions in your daily life since the last session?
2. Hand back the thought cards. What are your feelings about doing the thought card activity? Do you understand its purpose?
3. How have you used what you are learning in your families? with your peers?

Summarize the information in this section for students so that they have an idea of what they will be learning in this session.

The purpose of this session is to help group members become aware of their biases—the values, experiences, and opinions that influence how they listen to others. These biases, which can be understood as "filters," affect what people hear and what they block out when listening to someone. Biases impinge on our ability to listen (versus merely hearing words), and filters may block out feelings as well as content. Increasing awareness of students' filters can help them become more effective listeners

Recognizing and overcoming filters is only part of becoming an effective listener. Specific ways to respond as a listener to another person will be described in the next session.

SECRET VISITOR INTERVIEW

Bringing an adult stranger to the group can be a powerful means of helping students practice using a variety of questions to establish a relationship with another person and of introducing the skill of listening. It also can serve to inform a school or community official about your program and demonstrate the skills your group is acquiring.

Before bringing in the guest, tell your students that they will be meeting someone they don't know well and that they are to ask questions of the guest in an attempt to get to know her or him. Review with them the four types of questions and the conversation guidelines. Urge group members to ask open-ended questions, and encourage them to take time to think about and formulate their questions. You may want to give students a few minutes to write some possible questions in their journals. Then bring the guest in and introduce her or him by name only. Allow 15 to 20 minutes for questions and answers.

When the questioning is finished, ask the guest to share anything else he or she might want to say about her- or himself, and allow the guest to ask questions of the group. Thank the guest for coming before he or she leaves.

Processing the Activity

1. How successful do you feel the group was in asking questions?
2. What was difficult about doing this activity?
3. What did you learn about the person?
4. What did you learn about the work this person does?
5. How do you think this person feels about young people? What told you that?
6. What other feelings did the person reveal?
7. What did you not learn about the person that you wished you knew?
8. How did you use free information to formulate other questions?
9. How much personal information did you receive from your questions?

Ask each student to write a short thank-you note to the guest for spending time with the group. Tell students you will collect their notes at the next session.

INTRODUCTION TO LISTENING

1. Ask group members how many consider themselves to be effective, genuine listeners? Although no one can be an effective listener all of the time, indicate that you are sure some of them are capable listeners much of the time. Ask those who think they are to explain why they think they are. Push for specifics. If someone says, "Because others have told me that I am," ask what he or she does that makes others think this. You want to have the students identify the ingredients of effective listening.
2. State that some group members may have said at one time or another, "My parents [teachers, friends] just don't listen to me." If so, what do those people do to make it seem like they are not listening? What would help students to know that a parent, teacher, or friend is listening?
3. Ask the group to define effective, or sincere, listening.
4. Ask the group what can interfere with good listening.

Elton Mayo, who has written books about listening, has said, "One friend, one person who is truly understanding, who takes the trouble to listen to us as we consider our problems, can change our whole outlook on the world."

The skill of truly listening, not just hearing words, is one we must learn in order to care for others. Listening is the ability to be with another person in that person's world, attempting to experience what he or she is feeling and helping to interpret what he or she is trying to communicate. It is also sharing what we think we have heard to check for misunderstandings or incomplete ideas. True listening can also be just letting another person talk without verbal response, using only our eyes or body posture as acknowledgment. Becoming this kind of listener takes practice. More than this, it takes wanting to listen, being more interested in the other person than in oneself, and putting aside, for the moment, one's concerns and anxieties to be able to concentrate on the other person.

A LISTENING EXPERIENCE: THE KRIS STORY

Explain that the group is going to do an activity similar to the telephone game. You need three volunteers to be listeners. One will stay in the room and two will leave the room while you read "The Kris Story" (see pages 54–55). After the first volunteer has heard the story, another volunteer is brought in and the first listener shares with this new listener what he or she heard. When that volunteer is finished, the last volunteer comes in and the second listener shares with the third listener. Finally, the last listener shares with the group what he or she heard. Tell the listeners that they are not allowed to ask questions of the one telling the story.

Instruct the rest of the group to listen for different messages transferred from one listener to another as each listener shares.

Note: As the leader, observe carefully, taking notes as you listen to each speaker. Use your notes to illustrate important points.

After each listener has heard the story, ask her or him the following two questions:
1. In one sentence, what was the most important thing you heard?
2. If you could ask questions about this story, what would they be?

When all listeners have listened, shared, and answered the two questions above, ask each the following questions:
1. Did you like Kris? Why or why not?
2. What made this activity difficult for you?
3. How were you trying to listen?
4. What distractions did you experience?

Ask group members what they heard or observed:
1. What information was missed consistently?
2. What kinds of information became distorted?
3. What information did the listeners consistently report with accuracy?
4. What did you hear listeners doing as they passed on information to others?
5. What feelings did the information giver express that contributed to distortion?

The Kris Story

Few teachers even noticed Kris until another assignment was not turned in, or she earned a D on her latest math or science test. This quiet, slightly overweight high school junior of Pacific Island and white heritage calmly went to class, spoke to few, and seldom called attention to herself by raising a hand to respond. She was no trouble in class except that her teachers felt unsuccessful in trying to challenge her. Testing records showed that Kris had above-average intelligence, but teachers were stumped on how to motivate her to use it.

But with orchestra the story was different. Kris held second chair in the viola section and had earned a place in the prestigious City Youth Orchestra. She could have been first chair, if she heeded her mother's constant reminders and practiced regularly at home. But why bother? By her own standards, she was good enough.

It surprised even her mother when Kris decided to take a drama class and repeatedly tried out for roles in school plays. Occasionally, she got small parts, which delighted her. But if she didn't get a part, she was content to help with stage settings or other tasks assigned to her.

Kris liked to read all kinds of literature, both classic and popular. Reading was her escape when practicing or completing homework was supposed to be on her agenda. The consequences never ruffled her peaceful composure. She did things at her own time and in her own way.

Her middle-class parents found it a struggle to live in this more affluent community. Her father taught at a local community college, and her mother worked occasionally as a nurse. Kris had an older sister, who had dropped out of high school before graduating. She had a baby and was living with the father in a nearby neighborhood. Kris's sister got in a lot of trouble during high school—with the school and her parents. Now, however, she seemed content with domestic life.

In contrast, Kris never used drugs, drank, or smoked. She attended a youth group at a local church and went to Mexico on a mission trip during one spring break. Most of the young people on the trip came from different high schools than Kris. With her dull, oversized clothes, and clumpy boots, Kris was almost invisible. Few boys or girls noticed her smooth, beige skin or beautiful brown eyes. But she did make a few friends in the group.

Her mother, determined that Kris would graduate, sought counseling for her daughter. Kris faithfully attended these sessions and seemed fond of her counselor. She confided about her family's quarrels over how much she ate, her poor grades, and her lack of communication. Kris didn't speak harshly about her mother, but she didn't show the same warmth that was obvious when she talked about her father.

During her senior year, Kris showed interest in going to college. Her counselor suggested looking into a small liberal arts college that specialized in music, with a well-known foreign-exchange program. This possibility and pursuit had some effect on Kris's grades and her relationship with her mother improved. The remaining question was, Would she get accepted?

Points to Make

1. Listening is not simply memorizing what another says. Conversations are often filled with less important facts and details, so what we want to listen for are the themes or relevant points a person shares. These may be "heard" by repeated reference to some thought or issue or by the feeling words that surround them. The first question asked of each listener refers to this point. Frequently, what the listener says is the most important thing that he or she heard is seldom passed on to the next listener.

2. Although the listeners were not allowed to ask questions, questioning is an important part of listening. It isn't allowed in this activity because you want only the same information from the profile shared with each listener. Asking for the information you don't know or have is evidence that you are listening, and these questions often help the one talking to better understand her- or himself as well as tell her or his story.

3. When we begin to listen, certain information may trigger connections to ourselves, others, or experiences we have had. When this happens,

the mind may begin to categorize what is being said according to these events or circumstances and may cause the listener not to hear critical information unique to the speaker. Impressions of Kris may affect what the listener remembers or her or his interpretation of what was shared.

These experiences, impressions, categories, and interpretations come together to create a **listening filter.** This filter can cause us not to hear certain types of information and to exaggerate other information. Many people may remember only negative things about Kris and qualities she's lacking; others may pick up on her many positive traits. Effective listeners need to recognize the bias of their filters and make adjustments accordingly.

4. The volunteer listeners know the group is friendly, but when asked to listen in front of the group with all eyes turned on them, they can get nervous. This helps to illustrate that when we are anxious, *static*, or interference, can affect our listening capabilities. This makes it more difficult to focus on the person speaking and to hear the important message being shared.

LISTENING FOR ASSETS

After the discussion on listening, explain to the students that so far you have been reflecting on how the developmental assets can help you be a better peer helper. Now, you are going to work on identifying other people's assets. Ask group members to take out their copy of the 40 developmental assets and review them again. Ask the group to look at the assets while you read the profile of Kris once more. Their task is to identify Kris's assets based on what was read to them. Poll the students to see which assets and asset categories they can identify. Write the ones they name on the flip chart.

Invite the group to discuss Kris's assets based on the following questions:
1. How do you think she developed the assets she has?
2. What do you think kept her from becoming involved with risky behaviors such as those her sister did during high school?
3. Which assets does she seem to need most at this point in her life?
4. If Kris were a classmate of yours, what could you do to help her build more of the assets she needs?
5. Do you know anyone who is like Kris in your school?
6. How could listening be of help to someone like Kris?

Note after the activity that Kris did graduate from high school and was accepted at the liberal arts college she wanted to attend. While there, she made average grades as well as some good friends. During her junior year, she participated in an exchange program where she attended a school in Denmark. When she graduated from college, she got a job with the Vista program and lived in Russia where she learned to speak Russian. She returned home after a year and is doing social service work on the East Coast.

REFLECTING ON ASSETS

Ask students to think about what assets they built during this session. Assets they might mention include interpersonal competence, cultural competence, personal power, sense of purpose, caring, restraint, self-esteem, positive view of personal future, and youth as resources.

Explain that the story of Kris demonstrates that no one experiences assets in the same ways. People have different "power" assets (those assets that are most influential in their lives). We need to realize that someone else's life experiences with assets may not be the same as our own.

HOMEWORK ASSIGNMENT

1. Tell the students to continue practicing the use of open-ended questions and listening for the "free" information these questions provide for conversations.
2. Have students complete and bring in their thought cards or send an email you.
3. Ask group members to come prepared to share during the next session an important experience in their lives. They can define "important" any way they wish.
4. Ask students to start thinking of ways that young people can help build assets for and with their peers, rather than for themselves. The discussion about Kris may trigger some ideas. Ask the students to continue writing ideas for this list in their journals throughout the training. Tell them you will collect their lists at the end of the training.
5. Remind students to bring in their thank-you note for the secret visitor.

1. Prepare your secret visitor before the session by explaining what the students are practicing. Tell the visitor that he or she does not have to answer any question with which he or she is uncomfortable. Think about inviting a person whom you would like to have become more familiar with your program.

2. It's important always to act in asset-building ways. The questions in point 2 of the Introduction to Listening section provide a good opportunity for you to model respectful listening and caring about what is said in response to a question.

3. Have a few students take notes during the Kris listening experience. What information does the listener pass on? What words do the speakers use to share what they heard? What messages did these words convey to the next listener? Were these words repeated?

4. Asking each listener if they liked Kris helps to illustrate how filters work. If listeners didn't like Kris, they most likely heard and remembered more negative aspects of her personality. If they liked Kris, listeners probably heard and remembered more of her positive qualities.

5. Listeners tell you what was the most important piece of the Kris story. But the listener may not pass along this information to the next listener. If this happens, ask the student listener why. The response can illustrate the phenomenon of hearing information such as facts versus listening to themes and feelings expressed in conversations.

6. During the Kris listening activity, compare what the group heard to what the individual listeners heard. Differences can demonstrate what happens to our listening when we are nervous.

7. Her teachers were stumped about how to help Kris. If you have time in the session, have students volunteer ideas for how teachers could have helped build Kris's developmental assets.

8. Be prepared to deal with frustrations that result when one student does not "hear" what another has related to her or him. If this situation arises, it provides a good opportunity to discuss the importance of communication between two people, the influence of their filters, and how it feels to be "heard" or "not heard."

Communication Skills:
Listening for Content and Feelings

Leader's Goals
1. To teach students how to listen effectively for content and feelings
2. To demonstrate different ways of responding when trying to listen
3. To understand the power of a "feelings" vocabulary

Students' Skill Development
1. Practicing different ways to respond when listening
2. Using an expanded vocabulary for the expression of feelings

Leader's Tasks
1. To return thought cards with your comments, collect thought cards, and distribute blank thought cards
2. To collect thank-you notes to send to last week's visitor
3. To demonstrate four different listening responses

Materials Needed
1. A copy of the following for each group member:
   - Handout 9, Types of Responses
   - Handout 10, Statements for Listening Responses
   - List of feeling words collected during Session 4
2. Several dictionaries or thesauruses
3. Cards for thought card activity

Homework Review

Use this method for reviewing homework. Ask group members to think about how they used questions during contact with others since the last session. When the group has had enough time to think, pick someone to start. Ask her or him to tell the person on the left what they did. The person on the left then turns to the left and tells that person what he or she has done. Continue around the circle until all have shared. Congratulate those who have made efforts to practice this skill in their daily lives.

Choose a student leader for the next session's homework review.

SUMMARY OF THE PREVIOUS SESSION AND PURPOSE OF THIS SESSION

1. What did you learn from the previous session?
2. What was confusing about that session?

Collect the students' thank-you notes.

Summarize the following information for students as a guide for what they will be learning in this session.

The previous session focused on **listening filters** that affect what we do and do not hear. Now the focus is on how we show another person that we are listening by the responses we give. Real listening is a quest to discover the core of a message without judging. Especially when talking about a personal, emotional, or serious issue, many people don't know how to express what they really want to say. They may lack the vocabulary to put their feelings or thoughts into words, or they may be confused about what they want to say. An engaged, caring listener can help others sort out what they want to say, and in the process help those sharing learn more about themselves.

Obviously, many conversations are direct and uncomplicated. All we may need is just to hear the words: "I'm going to be home at nine P.M." "I can't do that because I have to work that day." "I have a brother and two sisters." But when we seek to develop a closer relationship or build a friendship, deeper exchanges and genuine listening are necessary. People tend to seek out others who are good listeners because instead of being judgmental, real listening affirms, clarifies, deflates conflict, and comforts.

This session is intended to teach types of responses we can use to accomplish this kind of in-depth listening. Only through practice can we learn to determine which type of response will be the most helpful for the particular situation or message. But even if we misjudge the appropriate response, the person speaking will know we are *trying* to listen and will continue the conversation. With enough practice, these responses become natural.

PRACTICING TYPES OF RESPONSES

Distribute Handout 9, Types of Responses, and review it with the students. After describing the four types of responses, make sure group members understand them. Ask if there are any questions.

Ask for two volunteer listeners. Then talk about a personal issue meaningful to you that the group will understand. Ask each listener to respond to you, using different types of listening responses. Perhaps the first asks a question. The second might pick out a phrase you used or provide a different interpretation. Respond to each listener. Then, share your reactions to these two listeners with the group.

Distribute Handout 10, Statements for Listening Responses, which gives examples of comments a person might make in a conversation. Ask group members to write a listening response using as many of the response types as they can.

When everyone has finished, ask for volunteers to read their responses as you go over each statement. Point out which response type their answers are. Then ask the following questions:

1. What did you notice about the difference in responses to the same statement?
2. Which statements were the most difficult to respond to? Why?
3. What feelings did you recognize in the statements?
4. What feelings do you think were overlooked?
5. Which type of response was used the most?
6. Which of these responses would be most effective in helping to resolve a conflict?

SHARING AN IMPORTANT EXPERIENCE

Remind group members that part of their homework assignment was to think of an important experience in their lives. Divide the students into threes to share this experience. Explain that they should take turns in the small group; one person starts by telling the other two about her or his experience. One of the two is to listen for the **content** (information) that is shared. The other is to listen for the **feelings** the speaker expresses. When finished, each shares what he or she heard about the content and feelings. Then the small group shifts roles and repeats the exercise, and then again, so that each person has the role of speaker, content listener, and feelings listener.

Processing the Activity

1. Which role was the most difficult?
2. How effective were your listeners?
3. How did it feel to be listened to this way?
4. What did you learn about yourself?
5. What feelings were expressed?
6. Which types of listening responses were used most frequently?
7. Which type of listening response was harder to feed back to the speaker? Why?

DEVELOPING A FEELINGS VOCABULARY

Feelings have a powerful influence on us, our knowledge of ourselves, our relationships with others, our understanding of others, our communication of messages, and our establishment of strong relationships. If we don't have the words to express our emotions, there is a part of ourselves that we don't know and cannot share.

Without an adequate vocabulary to express feelings, we often "group" many emotions under general words such as: *good, great, love, like, cool, smooth, scary, awesome,* and *awful.* Like umbrellas, these words cover a variety of the more specific emotions we really experience. These broad words also have different meanings for different people. Therefore, it is helpful to develop a feelings vocabulary that can specifically express what we are feeling, as well as help another person understand more accurately what we are trying to communicate.

1. Write on the flip chart some of the feelings words you have collected from previous activities and discussions, including those in the listening activity. Choose the ones most frequently used. Divide group members into pairs and assign several words to each pair.
2. Give each pair a dictionary or thesaurus. Ask them to look up synonyms for each of the words and then use the synonyms in a sentence to express a feeling that they will share with the group.
3. As each group shares, write the synonym next to the original word on the chart. Ask the group to study the two lists. What different meanings do the students get from the new word compared with the original one? Compared to the more general word, what different thoughts or images, if any, does the synonym bring to mind?
4. Have each person choose two new words from the lists to practice using in conversations before the next session or in what they write on their thought card.
5. End the session by having each student express some kind of appreciation for the person on her or his right, using one or more of the new vocabulary words. This can be about how much the student appreciates the person's sharing in the group, her or his mood, appearance, and so on.

REFLECTING ON ASSETS

Ask the students what they are learning about assets. Write these answers on the flip chart and have students record answers in their journals. Ask how the listening responses they have learned help build assets—their own and those of others. Have students record these answers in their journals as well. You can explain to the students that real listening helps them build interpersonal competence and caring because when you listen, you show another person that he or she is important to you. The one being listened to in turn feels valued, which builds self-esteem.

HOMEWORK ASSIGNMENT

1. Ask students to practice the use of listening responses in conversations with peers and family.
2. Have students write in their journals the new feelings words they learned in this session. Ask them to practice using some of these words in their conversations.
3. Remind group members to complete and return their thought cards.

1. The Statements for Listening Responses on Handout 10 are only examples. As the leader, you may want to prepare different comments that would be more relevant to your group.

2. As leader, you might read some of the Statements for Listening Responses aloud, using facial expressions, tones of voice, or hand gestures to convey feelings. Then have group members read some of the statements to themselves. You can explore which statements were easier to respond to. Most likely, your results will show that voice and nonverbal expressions add much more to what we hear while listening.

3. If you don't have enough time in the session for the Statements for Listening Responses activity, divide the statements, giving half to one group and the rest to the other. Everyone still gets practice but has fewer responses to write.

4. Be sure to use the feelings words collected from Session 4 in this feelings vocabulary activity.

5. As a reminder for how to be an asset role model for students during the training, review the sidebar on pages xiv–xv of the introduction.

Types of Responses

Posing a Question: This is perhaps the most useful response you can give if it deals with something significant that the person has said. It immediately indicates that you have "heard" some of what the person shared. The question can center on a word used in the conversation that could be interpreted various ways; on a phrase; or on a particular subject that was interjected while talking about a different topic.

1. **Word:** "You said it was *complicated*. What do you mean by complicated [weird, strange, meaningful]?" You may think you know what a word means, but you don't know what it means to the other person.

2. **Phrase:** "It was *the look she gave me* that bothered me." "We were sitting at the table *doing our usual thing,* when Dad got angry." What *was* the look given? What *is* doing the usual thing? Answers to these questions might clarify the real issue the person needs to discuss.

3. **Subject:** "We were talking about insurance coverage because of her operation, and because of my chest problems I was interested in what she had found out." *"Despite what my mother thinks,* I am very involved with this program and am spending a lot of time working on it." Asking about the chest problem might open the door to talking about a critical personal concern; finding out what the mother thinks could expand the conversation to a discussion of family problems.

Reflecting a Feeling: Feelings play an important part in conversations. However, people often overlook feelings conveyed by tone of voice, eye expression, hand movement, or body posture. The listener may be afraid to call attention to these feelings because he or she does not know what to do with them once they are acknowledged. And yet, these feelings could be exactly what the speaker wants you to "hear." When a listener *does* respond to feelings rather than words spoken, the speaker often expresses a sigh of relief, and gives a totally different "story" from the original one. The listening responses can be as simple as: "You sound sad." "You seem defeated." "I can tell you feel proud." "You seem worried." If your reading of the feelings is not correct, most often the person will say, "No, it's not that, but I *am* feeling . . ." The person may even say, "No, it's not that, but now I know what I *am* feeling."

Picking Up on a Thought or Issue: Sometimes when a person is talking about something, he or she keeps referring to an issue or thought, perhaps not even consciously. A listener who brings attention to this may make the conversation a deeper, more meaningful exchange. Here's an example: A friend is talking about a particular class she doesn't like. She keeps mentioning how the teacher treats certain students in the class and how the teacher handles discipline. A listening response might be: "You sound as though this teacher doesn't like you, and perhaps you're having a hard time in there because you're not getting the kind of help you need from her." This could provide your friend with the opening to talk about her lack of self-confidence, not only in this class, but also in other ways.

Responding with a Different Interpretation: This response is neither counseling nor a directive as to how the person should think. It provides a new, objective way of looking at things, especially when dealing with an emotional issue. Here's an example: A friend tells you that his dad doesn't like him, is always on his case, and lets his sister get away with everything. He says that because he had used up his allowance he didn't have money for the ski trip his friends had planned, and his dad wouldn't give him the money to go. Then, he overslept several mornings and was late to school because his dad wouldn't give him a ride. "He always gives a ride to my younger sister if *she's* going to be late!" Your response might be, "I think your dad *does* care about you. He cares enough to want you to learn from your mistakes and to understand the consequences of those mistakes. His actions tell me that he expects more from you than you do your-self. That's a compliment."

Statements for Listening Responses

◆ Going to a new school is hard, especially a private school where everyone is caught up in doing the teenage thing.

◆ The teachers aren't interested in me. They like the students who know the answers, put up their hands, look cool, and cozy up to them.

◆ My mother is too tired to talk to me. She works hard all day and just wants to watch TV in the evening when she gets home. All she wants is for me to stay out of trouble.

◆ I told Lisa in confidence who won the art contest. Our adviser had trusted me with the names, and they weren't supposed to be revealed until the awards assembly. Lisa told some of her friends, and then she went to our adviser and told her I had let it out of the bag. Lisa's saying I can't be trusted. I thought she was my friend. I'll never trust her again.

◆ Our school could be more caring if we didn't have so many cliques. You don't fit in if you don't wear the right clothes or have a cool boyfriend or girlfriend. Certain kids get away with all kinds of things. Their parents have more pull with the administration than parents who have less money or lower positions in the community. Some kids never get chosen for teams or activities. This school should be more fair.

◆ We pretty much get to do what we want in my family. It doesn't matter what time we come in at night. My parents never seem to mind what grades I bring home, and they don't bug me if my room is messy or about what I wear to school. They want to be friends, so they don't criticize what I do and give me lots of freedom.

◆ I'm not sure I ever want to get married. It's a big strain to live with someone year after year. You can't do your own thing and develop your own talents if you have to adjust to another person's desires. My mother didn't go to graduate school because my dad wanted to start a business. Then they had my sister and me, and she was busy raising us. Why should someone cut off a career to get married and then get mad about it because he or she has to do other things?

Assertiveness Skills: Expressing Rights and Desires

Leader's Goals

1. To help students identify stressful relationships
2. To identify for students three methods of responding if treated unfairly or denied rights

Students' Skill Development

1. Expressing right or desires with positive, assertive communication techniques
2. Using the Assertiveness Guidelines to guide response to others

Leader's Tasks

1. To return thought cards with your comments, collect thought cards, and distribute blank thought cards
2. To share an experience that demonstrates being assertive
3. To discuss and illustrate the responses: Passive, Aggressive, Assertive

Materials Needed

1. Flip chart and easel
2. A copy of the following for each group member:
   • Handout 11, The Three Methods of Responding
   • Handout 12, Assertiveness Guidelines
3. Cards for thought card activity

Homework Review

Ask the student leader to begin discussion on the group experience using listening responses in conversations with peers and family. Write on the flip chart the new feelings words group members used in these conversations.

Have the student leader select someone to guide the next session's homework review.

SUMMARY OF THE PREVIOUS SESSION AND PURPOSE OF THIS SESSION

1. Which of the listening responses did you find most useful in your conversations?
2. What part of the session on listening would you like to review to help you be better listeners?

Give students an overview of this session by summarizing the following information.

A basic skill students need to be peer helpers is to have the confidence to speak out when they or their peers are not valued or treated with dignity, or when something they value is neglected. This skill is assertiveness, and it affects a variety of interpersonal situations—this session will focus on dealing with authority figures.

Assertiveness is a word frequently used to indicate a way of behaving in a variety of everyday situations. These include standing up to peer pressure, being confident in negotiations, sharing opinions in controversial discussions, or asking to be treated respectfully. Often, the word carries a negative image of brashness, dominance, or selfishness. Actually, assertiveness means to state or express positively something of importance or value to the person exercising it. By doing so, we are being honest with others and with ourselves. An assertive person is not trying to *win* at the expense of another, nor trying to put another down. Rather, such a person is modeling *dignity*, which is one way to help peers acquire this valuable skill. Therefore, learning how to be assertive without being arrogant, rude, or disrespectful is an important skill for peer helpers to acquire.

Learning to be assertive starts with a belief that we have a right to express our desires and values despite what others say or do. To have such self-confidence, we have to know our desires and values. Do we want to be treated differently by others? Do we value what others think about us more than we value ourselves? Are we willing to risk being cut from our group for standing up for what we believe is right? We must thoughtfully answer questions such as these to find the confidence needed to act assertively.

Assertiveness also requires an understanding of how tone of voice, body language, and word choice can determine the responses we receive from others. The calmness of our voice, lack of aggressive body movements, such as finger pointing, and the firmness of carefully chosen words alert others to listen. These aspects may also convince others to accept our position.

Assertiveness is important in three different types of interpersonal situations: (1) dealing with people in authority; (2) handling peer pressure; and (3) talking about sensitive issues. Each of these situations requires different strengths and motivations that affect our ability to act assertively. Therefore, each of the situations will be covered in individual sessions.

IDENTIFYING STRESSFUL RELATIONSHIPS

Ask students to think of authority figures with whom they have contact throughout a normal week—parents, teachers, caregivers, bosses, coaches. Do some of these people treat them in ways that seem unfair or are embarrassing, or that make life difficult? Have them think about how they handle these situations. What do they do or say? Give the students time to think. Then you as leader offer to share a personal example to demonstrate what you are asking of them. When you are finished, ask a volunteer to start and proceed around the circle. As students share, take notes on how they respond in these situations. When all have finished, summarize their behaviors by writing them on the flip chart.

Then lead a discussion using some of the following questions:
1. How did you feel about the way you acted or responded?
2. How successful were your actions or behaviors?
3. Why do you think you were/are treated this way?
4. What could you do to influence how you are treated?
5. What keeps you from telling this person how you want to be treated?

Using some of the examples group members have shared, ask a few to demonstrate their situations. As leader, take the role of the authority figure, responding as you think you might in each situation. After each demonstration, ask the group to evaluate what the student said or did and what resulted from this encounter.

THREE METHODS OF RESPONDING

Distribute Handout 11, The Three Methods of Responding. Explain to the students that when people feel they are being treated unfairly or that their rights are being denied, they can respond in three different ways. Use examples from the demonstrations to illustrate these methods. If someone from the previous enactments demonstrated an assertive response, highlight this by pointing out the assertive words and behaviors. If not, take one of the situations and demonstrate what would have been an assertive response.

ASSERTIVENESS GAINS AND LOSSES

Often students agree that they would like to be assertive, but many are convinced that they can't do it or fear what might happen if they do. Students need to recognize and name these fears and become aware of what they may lose if they do not act assertively. Have them think about their situations by asking questions such as the following:
1. What keeps you from asking for what you desire or want in this relationship?
2. What do you stand to lose by accepting negative treatment?
3. What does the authority figure gain when you let her or him treat you this way?
4. What might you gain by speaking up for yourself in these situations?

List on the flip chart the things students say keep them from being assertive. Then make a chart with two columns, one headed **Losses** and the other **Gains.** Based on the discussion, ask group members to name the gains and losses they experience when they are and are not assertive. Then record what students say are the possible gains for the authority figure when they are not assertive. Have the group evaluate these lists. What do they learn from them? Which list carries the most value to them, their relationships, and their futures? How can they overcome their fears of being assertive? How can they help their peers who have similar fears? Allow time for the students to work together as a group to answer these questions. Often a comment from a peer will help another student progress toward an answer.

PRACTICING WHAT THEY HAVE LEARNED

Distribute Handout 12, Assertiveness Guidelines, and review it. Ask group members to write a short script in their journals of what they would like to say to an authority figure with whom they are having a problem, or what they want this person to know but aren't sure how to say. This could be the same concern that they shared earlier or a more current one.

Divide the group into threes to take turns practicing their scripts. One person will be the authority figure; another, the one with the problem; the third will watch the interaction and share her or his observations about the effectiveness of the assertive approach. When finished with one practice, switch roles. Repeat again until everyone has had a turn at each role. When the practice is finished, process the activity.

Processing the Activity

1. How did it feel to express your concern assertively?
2. Now that you have practiced your approach, what would you do differently?
3. How did the authority person feel about the approach that was used?
4. What suggestions did the observer give?
5. How convinced are you that you could now approach the actual person and be assertive?
6. What about this approach do you still fear?

Ask if any students would be willing to practice their script before the entire group. Don't pressure anyone to do this, but do encourage students to try because if a relationship is important to them, the more they practice the easier it will be to take responsibility and be assertive.

Share with students that even if they are assertive, the authority figure might not change. However, acting assertively allows students to preserve dignity, and that's important in the long run because it helps them to develop self-esteem.

REFLECTING ON ASSETS

Before closing the session, ask students to take out their list of the 40 developmental assets. Ask them to identify which of the assets they think this lesson supports. If they don't mention integrity, responsibility, peaceful conflict resolution, and personal power, discuss how the lesson relates to these assets.

The last tip in Handout 12 suggests making sincere inquiries into a person's life in order to encourage her or him to be more understanding of you and your concerns. Share with students that this action can build the asset of caring for all concerned.

HOMEWORK ASSIGNMENT

1. Ask students to approach the person they wrote about in their script and to try being assertive in situations that arise with others throughout the following week. Ask them to record one such experience in their journals.
2. Remind group members to continue using feelings words that they learned in the preceding session in their conversations and even in their assertiveness approach.
3. Ask them to respond on their thought cards this week to the following quote from Carol Burnett:"Only I can change my life. No one can do it for me." Have the students bring in these thought cards.

1. The key issue in learning assertiveness is believing that we have a right to ask for equal treatment, opportunities, behavior, and respect no matter what our age or position. When a person is a subordinate, such as a student, child, or employee, what keeps that person from being assertive is not only a lack of knowing how or what to say, but also a fear of consequences. Negative consequences are real, and we have to measure these consequences against what we value most. However, we often exaggerate fears or uncertainty. This is why spending time on losses and gains to the self is critical to this session. Allow everyone to express their fears without refuting them, but emphasize what they stand to lose by giving in to those fears.

2. Lead group members to see the positive side of confronting a fear. Confronting the fear of rejection by being assertive might lead to respect and admiration; calling attention to a problem may bring about change in how things are done; being assertive with parents might encourage parents to listen more attentively and resolve family arguments. Emphasize that even if nothing changes about the issues, at least by being assertive students have gained self-respect.

3. It is important to help group members think through what they might say in their first try at being assertive. Choice of words is critical, as is owning the feeling one has about the situation. Writing out a script and hearing themselves express their feelings assertively gives students courage to be assertive in the real situation. Sometimes it helps to tape-record what they want to say so that they hear their words and tone of voice.

4. If your group is reluctant to use personal examples of problems with people in authority, you can use some of the following hypothetical situations to practice the assertive approach:

   • A mother has told a friend about her daughter's crush on the friend's son. The friend reveals to the daughter that she knows about the crush. The daughter is embarrassed and feels betrayed by the mother.

   • A teacher decides to extend the deadline for an assignment on the day that it is due because several students complained that they didn't have time to finish it. You stayed up most of the night to finish it and are angry that the teacher is giving in to those who didn't meet the deadline.

   • You have looked forward to attending a special concert with your friends and have saved money for the ticket. The afternoon of the concert your mother tells you that you need to stay home to baby-sit your younger brother because she and your father need to attend a social event. Your parents knew about your concert and how much you were looking forward to it. They have asked you in the past to adjust your schedule to baby-sit. You are angry and feel their expectations are unfair.

   • You are working in a fast-food restaurant because you need the money. Your class has planned a field trip you have been looking forward to. You ask for time off but are denied it. A coworker has just asked for time off to go on a trip with his family, and the boss allowed it. You feel you are being treated unfairly.

5. The Basic Tenets of an Assertive Philosophy is included in Session 10 as Handout 16. You may want to distribute and discuss it at this point.

The Three Methods of Responding

PASSIVE

Responding passively means giving in to others and never asking for your rights or expressing your feelings. This response avoids conflict but allows others to dominate and control you, leaving you with feelings of low self-esteem, as well as lack of respect from the person in control. Often you leave the situation resentful and angry, which may build up to a future outburst.

AGGRESSIVE

This response often involves using the word *you* in an attacking manner whether through speech or body movements. Sarcastic remarks, put-downs, and pushiness are employed to get your way, regardless of the feelings and rights of others. Frequently this type of interaction is accompanied by angry body gestures, such as pointing with a finger or clenching your fists. Often you say things you later regret but can't retrieve, leaving a feeling of guilt and shame.

ASSERTIVE

Responding to others with humble self-confidence, honestly expressing your rights and desires, firmly, but kindly, is being assertive. To be assertive, your message must clearly express "I feel . . . " statements. Assertiveness does not deny the other person's feelings or positions, but expresses simply, while looking the other in the eye, what your plans, desires, or decisions may be. When you act assertively, you feel proud of yourself and usually are even ready to accept a negative response or reaction from the other person. Consequently, you often earn respect, cooperation, and admiration.

Assertiveness Guidelines

1. Describe the act, critical issue, or situation. A person is not always aware of what he or she has done or said to upset you.

2. Say how you feel, starting with an "I feel . . ." statement, rather than "You did [said] . . ." "You" statements put other people on the defensive.

3. State what you want and why, clearly and simply. Again, the other person may not know how to correct the situation or how they are offending.

4. Allow the person to respond. He or she may have a legitimate reason for what he or she has said or done. If so, acknowledge this, but repeat how this lack of understanding affected you. However, you don't have to agree with how the person handled the situation.

5. If the person doesn't agree with your presentation of the problem, simply ask if he or she understands how you feel. If not, repeat your "I feel . . ." statement.

6. Be realistic about your expectations. Allow the person a way to save her or his dignity. Not all things can be changed. There may be circumstances that contributed to this situation, so be understanding.

7. Do not get derailed into anger or arguments by how the person responds. In these cases, walking away is a powerful message that shows dignity.

8. Use tone of voice and body posture that convey confidence and dignity. Look the other person in the eyes, stand or sit tall, but not rigidly, and refrain from body gestures that may express nervousness or anger. Talk quietly and unhurriedly. Smile, if this is genuine, when concluding the exchange.

9. You may not get what you want from this exchange, but you will feel more self-confident, and probably will find you are treated with new respect in subsequent relationships.

10. **Hint:** It is helpful to show a genuine interest in the concerns of your parent/teacher/boss other than in disputes. Sincerely asking a person about issues in her or his life may encourage her or him to be more understanding of you and your concerns.

SESSION

9

Assertiveness Skills: Dealing with Peer Pressure

Leader's Goals

1. To list and explain three factors that influence choices in responding to peer pressure
2. To help students identify values that are tested with negative peer pressure
3. To demonstrate ways to handle negative peer pressure assertively
4. To help students understand that peer pressure can also be positive
5. To have students create a list of personal values

Students' Skill Development

1. Practicing how to stand up to peer pressure
2. Learning to be a good role model for others

Leader's Tasks

1. To return thought cards with your comments, collect thought cards, and distribute blank thought cards
2. To share a personal peer pressure situation
3. To review the three types of peer pressure: **Neutral, Negative,** and **Positive**
4. To review and discuss the basic factors that influence peer pressure choices

Materials Needed

1. Flip chart and easel
2. Masking tape
3. A sheet of writing paper for each group member
4. A copy of Handout 13, Resistance Skills: Effective Responses to Negative Pressure for each group member
5. Cards for thought card activity

Homework Review

Ask the student leader to review the homework assignment with the group. If not covered by the leader, ask about experiences approaching someone in authority about an issue. How successful were students' efforts? How did they feel about themselves afterward? What effect, if any, did the thought card quote have on them during the past week?

The student leader should choose someone to conduct the next session's homework review.

SUMMARY OF THE PREVIOUS SESSION AND PURPOSE OF THIS SESSION

Review Handouts 11 and 12, which were distributed in the preceding session. Ask:

1. How do the responses of passive, aggressive, and assertive differ from one another?
2. How have students used the lesson on assertiveness to help their peers?
3. Which of the Assertiveness Guidelines seem the most helpful? Why?

Negative peer pressure is a well-known issue for today's young people. The purpose of this lesson is to learn what makes negative peer pressure so influential and how to deal with it constructively, as well as discuss how peer pressure can be positive.

Ask the group the following questions and give people time to write answers in their journals. After they are done writing, discuss the responses with the group.

1. What do you think of when you hear the term *peer pressure?*
2. What kinds of situations have you experienced when peers pressured you?
3. Is peer pressure more difficult to handle because of who is doing it, or because of the kind of thing a person or group is trying to get you to do? Why?
4. What might be different about being assertive in peer pressure situations than being assertive with people in authority?
5. In comparison to direct pressure, what kinds of subtle pressure do you experience, such as wearing certain clothes, listening to certain music, or learning the right slang or language?

Based on group members' answers, summarize their feelings and thoughts about the differences between being pressured by a group rather than an individual. Clarify their understanding of the difference between peer pressure and pressure from authority figures.

Points to Make

When responding to people in authority, *we* are usually the ones who initiate the contact, seeking to achieve certain changes regarding behavior, decisions, or rights. Assertively, we express our feelings and desires and our reasons for these requests. The results or consequences depend on the responses we get.

In negative peer pressure situations, we need assertiveness skills to respond *when others approach us.* This pressure may come as a surprise. Or it may subtly affect us by what we observe or assume in association with our peers. (For example, girls may watch the "popular" crowd to see what they wear and do in order to make some of their own personal choices. Boys may not want to cry in public.) The pressure comes from balancing our decision with whom or what we value. Assertiveness skills help us state what it is we do or do not want to do.

Share the following true story:

John was a slightly built student in grade 10, who had always wanted to be on the high school basketball team. He practiced endlessly at home after school and finally made the junior varsity team. John was awed by this accomplishment. As conversations emerged in the locker room, where team members boasted of their sexual conquests, it became known that John still was a virgin.

One night John's teammates invited him to a party. He was thrilled by this sign of acceptance. A faithful member of his church's youth group and part of a family that took their faith seriously, John had never been to a party with team friends. When he got to the party, John's team surrounded him and told him that they were sorry he had not had the advantage of "knowing" a girl and that they wanted to present him with a gift. At this point they brought out a girl, who looked bold as well as bewildered. The guys said they had asked her to be a gift to him tonight and pointed to the bedroom.

John stood there shocked, thinking about what the team would say and the ridicule he would be subjected to if he didn't go through with this. At the same time, he remembered his parents' trust and the values he had been taught. He wondered how he would feel about himself if he used the girl in this way. He blinked, sweated, and reflected while the guys laughed and urged him on. Finally, he stammered out, "I can't do this," and headed toward the door. Silence followed. Then slowly, several other guys followed him, saying, "I haven't done it either." No mentions of the incident were reported in the school halls the following day.

After reading this story, lead the group to think about negative peer pressure by asking the following questions:
1. What kinds of peer pressure were exercised that night?
2. What was at stake for John?
3. What did he stand to lose or gain?
4. What influenced his choice?
5. What would you have done in a similar situation?

WHAT DOES PEER PRESSURE INVOLVE?

Peer pressure usually is viewed as negative. *Merriam-Webster's Collegiate Dictionary* defines pressure as "the application of force to something by something else in direct contact with it." In human terms, peer pressure means that a person or a group of people the same age is trying to get you to do something. There are actually three kinds of peer pressure: **Neutral, Negative,** and **Positive.**

Neutral pressure pertains to doing things that seemingly have no long- or short-term effect on one's life or that of others. Pressure to wear certain clothing and hairstyles would fall into this category.

Negative pressure involves risk-taking behaviors and actions that can be harmful to one's physical or emotional self. Negative peer pressure happens when peers try to convince other peers that an action is the "norm" and they should do it to be normal. Pressure to have sex or to use alcohol or other drugs belongs in this category.

Positive pressure can be an action or example that brings out the best in another person or group. Peer helpers exercise positive peer influence by taking courageous stands and opposing cruel words or acts against others, by not spreading gossip, and by reaching out to people left out of the group. Positive pressure is similar to positive peer influence.

Three basic factors influence our choice when faced with peer pressure:
1. Whom and what we value
2. Our vulnerabilities—for example, being lonely, needing acceptance, being impressed by someone, wanting status or power
3. Our willingness to do something to get what we think we want

To know how these factors will affect us, we need to be tested by peer pressure. Peer pressure challenges who we are, as a person, as a friend, as a member of a family and community. As someone once said, "My name I know. Who I am, I'm not sure." Responses to peer pressure demonstrate answers to the question of who we are, despite what our words may say. We need this testing to discover our true selves. This testing continues throughout life, regardless of age or circumstance.

VALUES AND VULNERABILITIES

Have students take out their journals and make three lists: **Whom do I value? What do I value?** and **How am I vulnerable** (most susceptible to giving in)? Ask them to write answers to these questions under each heading. You may want to give them examples of something you would put under each heading. While group members are writing, post three sheets of flip chart paper on the wall with the same headings. When they finish their lists, have the students circulate around the room, writing down items from their lists onto the flip chart pages. Tell them to add their own value, person, or vulnerability even if it duplicates others. Participate in this activity, adding items from your own list. When everyone is finished, ask for students' reactions and observations.

1. What are common items?
2. How many of you indicated that you valued yourself?
3. What kinds of situations or needs are most common as vulnerabilities?
4. How could you help one another be less vulnerable?

EXPERIENCING NEGATIVE PEER PRESSURE

Pass out sheets of paper. Ask group members to write a script of a negative peer pressure situation they have experienced, describing the situation, location, who was pressuring (leaving out specific names), and what pressure was exerted. Do not have them write their names on the page. Collect the papers and put them in a basket.

Choose someone to pick a page from the basket. He or she will then pick someone to be the person experiencing pressure. The student doing the pressuring can provide some background for her or his partner, taken from what was provided on the paper but without giving away the pressure's focus. Often, we are caught off guard when we are pressured, so you want to simulate this surprise. The one doing the pressuring should use any way he or she can to exert the pressure. The practice ends when the partner decides what he or she will do.

Repeat the enactment following the same procedures with two other students. If the group is small, give everyone a turn at pressuring and being pressured. If large, break into small groups so that everyone can experience enacting a scenario. Choose two or three examples to share with the entire group. If not all the situations are enacted, read those remaining so that students know what the other situations were.

Processing the Activity

1. How did it feel to pressure someone else?
2. What did you learn about yourself while pressuring the other person?
3. How real was receiving the pressure for you?
4. What did you learn about yourself as you experienced negative peer pressure?
5. Which situations were the hardest to resist?
6. What were the most effective ways to resist, based on your observations?
7. How might this practice help you in your daily life?
8. How often do you try to pressure others negatively?

EFFECTIVE WAYS OF DEALING WITH NEGATIVE PEER PRESSURE

If students have demonstrated effective ways to deal with negative peer pressure, write these on the flip chart and ask the group to brainstorm other ways. Then distribute Handout 13, Resistance Skills: Effective Responses to Negative Pressure, and go over it with the group.

Someone said, "Saying no is the ultimate act of personal control." When you're being assertive with an authority figure, you express and explain your feelings. When someone is pressuring you negatively, you don't have to explain because you are not asking that person to change her or his behavior. Instead, you are stating assertively what you do or do not want to do, and knowing whom and what you value gives you the power to say no whenever you want.

REFLECTING ON ASSETS

Ask students to identify the developmental assets that the skills in this session can help them build for themselves. Answers you can expect to hear include positive peer influence, responsibility, resistance skills, restraint, integrity, self-esteem, and personal power.

Then ask students to think about assets and how they can help them in negative peer pressure situations. Discuss the assets John had or used that helped him in his situation. In the peer pressure activity, did having assets help group members resist pressure? How?

Explain that by resisting negative peer pressure they may be giving their peers the courage to do so as well. This is *positive* peer pressure, and it's a way to build assets for others by being a positive peer influence.

To close, discuss assets in relation to values and vulnerabilities. Which assets could help group members feel less vulnerable and why?

HOMEWORK ASSIGNMENT

1. Tell students to pay particular attention to both obvious and subtle ways they are pressured throughout the week and how they pressure others—whether neutrally, negatively, or positively. Have them pay particular attention to situations in which they practice or observe positive peer pressure. Ask them to record their observations in their journals.
2. Ask group members to bring in or email thought cards related to how positive peer influence has affected them.
3. Remind students to keep observing the person to whom they were assigned and to record these observations in their journals.

1. At this point in the training, students leading the homework review should be sufficiently aware of the types of questions to ask about the homework. The questions included during the homework review portion of this session are important points to raise if the student leader does not mention them.

2. If you are using this training in a middle school setting in which discussion of sexuality is not appropriate, use a different story to illustrate dealing with negative peer pressure.

3. Although the emphasis in this session is on dealing with negative peer pressure, it is critical to highlight positive peer influence. This is a basic behavior you want to encourage as the students become peer helpers. In John's story, by his refusal to go through with using a girl, he not only resisted negative peer pressure, but also exerted positive influence. The boys who walked out with him felt the courage to be honest and perhaps taught the others something positive as well. Explain that positive peer pressure is similar to being a role model, which falls under the asset of positive peer influence. As one person said, being a positive role model is "standing in the gap." Once someone is standing in the gap, it makes it easier for the next person to continue filling in the space.

4. The more you draw on the experiences of your group members for discussions and activities, the more relevant the training will be, and the more they will apply what they are learning in their own lives.

5. Continue to review the sidebar on pages xiv–xv of the introduction so that you can serve as an asset role model for students throughout the training.

Resistance Skills: Effective Responses to Negative Pressure

1. Get the attention of the person(s) doing the negative pressuring:
- Use her or his name.
- Make eye contact when speaking to the person.
- Say, "Please listen to me!"

2. State your "no" decision:
- Use "I" message.
- Use a firm voice.
- Reinforce your message with body language.

3. When pressured:
- Use self-control.
- Restate your "no" decision.
- Suggest an alternative subject, if appropriate.
- Leave/walk away.

4. Try other ways to say no.
- Use humor.
- Change the focus.
- Reverse the pressure in a positive direction.
- Repeat yourself as often as necessary.
- Delay your response.
- Recruit help.

Assertiveness Skills: Managing Sensitive Issues

Leader's Goals
1. To demonstrate the skill of speaking to others about sensitive issues
2. To help students understand that when troublesome behaviors are left unresolved or handled ineffectively, they can affect interpersonal relationships

Students' Skill Development
1. Practicing effective ways of talking to another person about offensive, upsetting, and self-defeating behaviors
2. Sharing feelings without judging or attacking
3. Recognizing that dealing effectively with sensitive issues helps make a relationship healthy

Leader's Tasks
1. To return thought cards with your comments, collect thought cards, and distribute blank thought cards
2. To introduce guidelines for handling sensitive issues and detours
3. To illustrate the application of these two sets of guidelines

Materials Needed
1. A copy of the following for each group member:
   • Handout 14, Sensitive Issues Guidelines
   • Handout 15, Effective Ways to Handle Detours
   • Handout 16, The Basic Tenets of An Assertive Philosophy
2. Cards for thought card activity

Homework Review

Ask the student leader to guide the discussion on experiences with negative, neutral, or positive pressure that group members have had in the past week. Highlight the accounts of students who mention how the last session helped them deal with these experiences. Ask if any group members had opportunities to exert **positive peer influence** by modeling an act of caring, speaking up for an issue, or encouraging others to be more caring. Ask if they tried to exert negative peer pressure on anyone during the past week. As they did this, did they think about the training?

The student leader should designate someone to conduct the homework review for the next session.

SUMMARY OF THE PREVIOUS TWO SESSIONS AND PURPOSE OF THIS SESSION

In your own words, share the following information with students so that they are aware of what they will be focusing on in this session.

This is the third session on assertiveness skills. In the first session, we worked on how to speak up for our feelings and rights in dealing with people in authority. In the second session, we focused on types of peer pressure, primarily negative peer pressure, and we discussed three factors that influence how we respond to peer pressure.

Now we are going to look at being assertive with people you need or want in your life by resolving potential conflicts that could result in broken relationships. This critical relationship skill is one that many people never learn or practice. This skill also conveys to others that you are a person who can be trusted and respected.

Peer helping consists of many actions and ways of helping and serving others. Few people think of *constructive feedback,* frequently construed as criticism, as a peer-helping skill. But this neglected interpersonal skill often is the missing link needed to help change behaviors that interfere with desired personal relationships.

Establishing trust in a relationship and helping another person work through a problem are basic peer-helping skills. However, if you can't go a step further, when needed, to talk about negative behaviors that need changing, you may fall short of helping someone who requires honest feedback. Therefore, the skill of dealing with sensitive issues is vital—not only in helping those with problems, but also in dealing with upsetting behaviors that you experience from those around you. This session focuses on this peer-helping skill.

You show integrity and how much you value another person by your ability to honestly and calmly, but firmly, tell people how their behavior is affecting you and your relationship. Learning how to handle sensitive issues can help you avoid conflict that could lead to harsh words and even the end of a relationship.

IDENTIFYING SENSITIVE ISSUES

Read one or both of the following scenarios:

Jason and Frank

Jason and Frank have been friends since middle school. Now they are college classmates starting their sophomore year. Jason lives on campus, while Frank shares an apartment with other guys off campus. During the summer, Jason bought a car with the money he had earned at a summer job and was delighted to drive Frank and other friends around town to various events. Frequently, he gave rides to Frank to and from campus. He even lent his car to Frank when he had a special date or wanted to go to an event that Jason was not attending. However, Frank never offered to pay for gas or share the expense of the car, even though he used it frequently. What upset Jason even more was that sometimes Frank brought the car back with the gas tank almost empty.

Friday night Frank had used the car. The next morning when Jason left for an important appointment, he found the gas gauge on empty. Having to stop for gas made him late for his appointment. Driving home, he fought with his anger. He liked Frank and enjoyed his company. They had had lots of good times together. But Jason wondered if Frank liked his car more than him, and he was tired of being used in this way. They were going to meet for a study session later that afternoon, and Jason was determined to talk to Frank about the situation.

Kathy and Maria

Kathy had reached out to Maria when she moved from Mexico to their school in California. She helped Maria get settled and showed her around the school, introducing her to her friends and suggesting activities Maria might enjoy where she could meet other friends. In the process, they spent quite a bit of time together and began confiding in one another. Eventually, however, much of their conversations revolved around Maria and her problems and complaints. Although she spoke quite good English, she felt kids made fun of her accent. She said she was excluded from social events because she didn't have the "right" clothes, even though she dressed well and had a beautiful smile. She frequently called Kathy at night while Kathy was trying to do homework. Maria would complain about teachers, how she was treated in class, or something that had come up during the day. Kathy listened and tried to present an objective version of what Maria was telling her, but it was taking a tremendous toll on her time and energy.

Last night, when Kathy was trying to study for an important calculus test, Maria called again. Kathy told her that she was studying and didn't have time to talk. Maria responded, accusing Kathy of not being a real friend. Kathy tried to reassure Maria that she did care about her and finally was able to end the conversation. When she went back to her room, Kathy found it hard to study. She was angry that Maria did not trust her friendship and angry about the amount of time Maria was demanding of her. She did not want to cut her off, but the friendship seemed to be only going Maria's way, and Kathy was no longer getting much satisfaction out of it. She was afraid if she talked to Maria about this, Maria would take it as another racial rejection. What should Kathy do?

 What are group members' impressions of the people in these stories? Do they know people who have behaviors or personalities similar to these four? Which of the four do they find more appealing? Why?

Ask someone to take the role of Jason and another to take the role of Frank. Ask these students to enact what Jason might say to Frank when they meet in the afternoon. When the dialogue has progressed sufficiently, have the group process what was gained or lost through the conversation. What was resolved? How will this conversation affect the two friends' relationship? What helped? What didn't help? How relevant is this situation to things group members have experienced in their lives? **Do not suggest better ways to deal with this situation.** You will return to this story later.

Turn to the story of Kathy and Maria. Ask group members what they think Kathy should do. If they suggest that Kathy talk to Maria, again ask for volunteers to enact that conversation, asking questions similar to the ones that followed the Jason and Frank story. If group members don't feel Kathy should talk to Maria, ask how their solutions would solve the problem. What might be the consequences to their relationship? What would be gained or lost from these solutions. **Do not try to convince them that Kathy should talk to Maria.** Return to this story later.

Using examples that emerge from the discussion of these two stories, make the transition to sensitive issues in the students' lives.
1. How many of you have a friend or family member who has a habit that upsets you? Is this something the person might be able to change if he or she chose to?
2. How have you tried to let this person know about this upsetting behavior and how it affects you?
3. If you haven't talked to the person about this, why haven't you?
4. What might happen to this relationship if you either wait too long to do something about what upsets you or you avoid doing anything?

PRACTICE TALKING ABOUT A SENSITIVE ISSUE

Ask each person to think of someone he or she needs to talk to because there is something upsetting in their relationship. Some students may not be able to think of a particular person. Ask these students to think of some upsetting behavior they have observed in others to use during the practice session.

Explain that you are not talking about trivial habits, such as always borrowing your lipstick or leaving empty soda cans in your locker. You're talking about habits that are harder on a relationship, such as people not showing up when they said they would or keeping others waiting because they are running late. These types of habits show disrespect for you and your time.

Divide the group into pairs. One partner begins by telling the other who he or she is (i.e., a classmate, sister, boyfriend, coworker, neighbor). Then this partner introduces the upsetting issue and talks about it. The other partner plays the friend and should respond naturally to what her or his partner says. Further conversation might follow this exchange before you ask the students to stop. After 10 minutes, reverse roles, with the partner who played the friend now presenting her or his upsetting issue.

Processing the Activity

1. What approaches were used to introduce the sensitive issue?
2. Did the *friend* understand your upsetting behavior?
3. What feelings did the *friend* have while receiving this message?
4. What messages did the *upset friend* send talking about this issue? Was it criticism? concern? sincerity? kindness? threats?
5. What suggestions, if any, were given for modifying the behavior? Were these realistic and/or possible?
6. What did you learn from practicing these conversations?
7. What skills did you use?

Points to Make

Up to this point, you have not made any specific suggestions for handling these issues skillfully and kindly, either in the enactments with Jason and Frank and Kathy and Maria or in the pairs' practice sessions. The reason for this is to have the students experience various approaches and reactions that are either helpful or unhelpful. You undoubtedly now have many examples to use to illustrate the importance of each of the guidelines you will now introduce.

GUIDELINES FOR HANDLING SENSITIVE ISSUES AND DETOURS

Distribute Handout 14, Sensitive Issues Guidelines. Review the steps for talking with someone about a sensitive issue. Demonstrate each step by rewording phrases used during the Jason-Frank enactment or in shared discussion of the paired practice sessions.

Before doing a second practice session, introduce Handout 15, Effective Ways to Handle Detours. Explain that even though you prepare to talk to friends using the guidelines, others may still not want to hear what you have to say. They may, consciously or unconsciously, use various "detours" to steer the conversation off track. Engaging a person in an argument is the most universal detour. It helps to be prepared for such detours and to know how to respond when they happen.

Distribute Handout 15. Call on different students to read the detours. Answer and put appropriate emotion or feeling into your response. Ask for any questions or comments about the list when you have finished and before moving into the final practice session.

FINAL SENSITIVE-ISSUE PRACTICE

Ask group members to return to their original partners. This time, using the two handouts and what they have learned, students repeat their practice conversations. Before asking students to begin, give them time to read the handouts and think through what they now want to say or do. Students might choose to focus on a different issue during this second practice session.

Processing the Second Practice

1. What was different about this approach?
2. What was difficult or uncomfortable about using this approach?
3. What different feelings did the *friend* experience compared to the first practice?
4. What different responses to the messages were demonstrated?
5. How might this approach affect the future of this relationship?

Points to Make

1. We need to examine whether the upsetting behavior is affecting many of this person's relationships. We need to ask ourselves, Is this behavior affecting only us or others as well? If the problem affects only us, then we should honestly reflect on how much we contribute to the problem before discussing it.
2. We have to care about the person or the relationship to risk talking about a sensitive issue. Such a conversation involves considerable emotional energy, and despite how skillfully we approach the issue, the conversation may result in misunderstanding.
3. The behavior in question should be one that a person could change if he or she chose to do so. For example, Frank could choose to bring the car back filled with gas, but he hasn't.
4. We may hesitate to bring up the topic for fear of hurting the other person, but not dealing with it may hurt our relationship more severely in the long run. Feelings do not go away unless expressed, and upsetting feelings not dealt with may finally come out as words and actions that are truly harmful.
5. A person may be unaware that her or his behavior is upsetting. If so, the person hasn't had the choice of changing. Dealing with a sensitive issue can be an act of love and concern when handled carefully— even if the person decides not to modify her or his behavior.
6. Merely telling a person what bothers us is not sufficient. Often he or she will not know how else to act. Always accompany the pointing out of upsetting behaviors with helpful suggestions of desired behaviors.
7. Thinking we don't have the right to be upset will not erase the feelings we have. We have to reframe our thinking. Denying a person our feelings or expressing them as attacks only hurts the person. We have a right to express our feelings—kindly and clearly.
8. The simple shift of pronouns turns a criticism of another person to a declaration of our feelings. "You are . . . " is a criticism. "I feel . . . " is a feeling statement.
9. Always choose a time when this conversation will not be interrupted or hurried. Use a serious tone of voice to alert a friend to the conversation's importance.

10. Friendships often are tested by a person's willingness to either give or receive constructive feedback on behaviors that, if changed, would improve the ability to make and keep satisfying friendships and relationships.

Return to Jason-Frank and Kathy-Maria

If there is time, ask for volunteers to reenact the scene between Jason and Frank. If time is limited, spend a few minutes talking about how Jason might now be able to handle the encounter effectively. If you don't have time to discuss Jason and Frank, do spend time discussing how Maria's ethnic background affected Kathy's response to the situation. Are we being kind to someone of another color or culture if we withhold constructive feedback? If the members of the group are culturally or ethnically diverse, invite individuals to share their thoughts about how exploring these differences can help the group grow and increase its cultural competence.

REFLECTING ON ASSETS

When you are assertive about a sensitive issue, you exercise your personal power by letting others know how you feel. Handling sensitive issues also helps you build interpersonal competence. It is a skill you can apply and teach to others to help them develop the asset of peaceful conflict resolution.

Ask the following questions to help students reflect on assets as they relate to this session:

1. Do you see other ways that dealing with a sensitive issue could help build assets, either your own or someone else's?
2. What assets would be helpful to possess in order to work through such issues with friends?
3. What do we need to know about another's culture or other diversity to avoid offending them, but still assist in building their assets?

HOMEWORK ASSIGNMENT

1. Urge group members not to put off approaching a friend, family member, or coworker with whom they may be having a problem. Since they have just practiced assertiveness skills, it is an opportune time to do this. Suggest that students may want to write out a "script" of what they want to say and practice it. Group members may even record themselves so that they can hear how this might sound to the person they are approaching. Rehearsing in front of a mirror would help them study their facial expressions.
2. Remind them to fill out and return their thought cards or send an email to you.

1. It is suggested that you not process the initial scenarios of Jason and Kathy with the group. However, issues relevant to what you want to teach may come up during the discussion of either of these two situations. If this occurs, go with the timing. This is particularly true of Kathy and Maria's scenario, which is intended to open up discussion of the cultural competence asset. Whether this discussion takes place at the beginning or end, make sure you allow time for it.

2. Handout 16, The Basic Tenets of an Assertive Philosophy, is included in this lesson. You may want to distribute and discuss this list as a conclusion to the three sessions on assertiveness, or you may want to use it in one of the previous two sessions. If you distribute this handout here, tell students that it summarizes the points covered in all three sessions and can serve as a reminder for them to use assertiveness in their lives.

Sensitive Issues Guidelines

Tell the person with whom you want to discuss an issue that you would like to talk with her or him about a matter that is important to you. Ask when a convenient time would be. If the person wants more information at this point, simply say, "I would rather not get into it until we can have our talk." Make yourself available at her or his convenience. At the appointed time, follow these steps:

Step 1. Describe the Upsetting Behavior

Approaching the person shortly after he or she has demonstrated the behavior—not two weeks later—is best. The behavior should be something you have personally observed or experienced, not something reported to you by another person. Be specific and concrete.

Example: Last night when you returned my car, the gas gauge read empty. I had to stop for gas this morning, making me late for my appointment. This is the third time this month that you have used my car and returned it without filling up the tank.

Step 2. Express Your Feelings about This Behavior

Feelings are best expressed with "I" statements rather than "it" or "you" statements.

Example: "I feel angry and taken advantage of because of my generosity in letting you use my car."

Step 3. Explain the Reason for Your Feelings

Give the person a concrete reason for your feelings to help her or him understand them.

Example: "I feel angry, not only because you frequently bring back the car with an empty tank, but also because you never offer to buy any gas when I give you or your friends rides."

Step 4. Specify the Behavior You Want

How do you want the person to behave differently? Describe specifically what you want the person to do. Vagueness seldom produces results.

Example: "I want you to always put some gas in the car after you have used it for an outing when I'm not along. I also want you to agree to contribute ____ per month for the cost of the gas I use to give you rides."

Step 5. Specify Consequences

Often a person feels that articulating consequences is the same as making threats, but there are always consequences for what we do or don't do. Not discussing consequences does not prevent them from happening. Consequences can be positive as well as negative. Because positive consequences have the most powerful effect, you should state them first.

Example: (**Positive**) "If you will agree to this plan, I will be happy to continue to give you rides and loan you my car. I will also continue to enjoy our friendship."

(**Negative**) "If you don't agree, I will no longer lend you my car and only give you rides when it is convenient for me.

When communicating consequences, discuss only those you are willing and able to carry out. You put your credibility at risk if you talk about a consequence that you fail to enforce. Therefore, to convince the other person to change behavior, you should clearly decide consequences before the conversation. This is especially true in identifying positive consequences. What you consider positive may seem unimportant to the other person. However, never underestimate the power of a sincere compliment or constructive offer in helping another person value your friendship, opinion, and regard.

The tone of voice used to express your message is very important. Speaking in a whining, complaining, angry, or apologetic tone can make the other person defensive and can detract from the seriousness of your words. When conveyed in a firm, clear, and calm voice and manner, your words call attention to the significance of the issue and message.

Effective Ways to Handle Detours

People often don't want to hear your message, or they want to justify their behavior. So, they may try to sidetrack you. Recognizing common detours can help you respond more effectively and be more successful in having your message heard.

Common Detours		Your Response
Delaying:	*Not now. I don't have time.*	*When do you have time?* Be accommodating but assertive.
Distracting:	*You have such a pretty smile when you talk.*	*Thank you! Now, let's talk about this important issue.* Listen, but don't forget your point.
Denying:	*That's not true. I really am interested.*	*I disagree. I feel . . .* Persist by repeating your message.
Attacking:	*You're always so serious. You never want to relax.*	*If by "serious" you mean I want to get this plan finished, then, yes, I am serious.* Redefine a negative label.
Blaming:	*If you were better organized, we wouldn't have to have so many meetings.*	*What exactly do you mean by "better organized?"* Urge the person to rephrase a vague criticism as an explanation.
Threatening:	*If you don't stop criticizing me, I'll just resign from this board.*	*Let's talk about this later.* Don't pursue the conversation now. Ignore this type of detour, and walk away.
Debating:	*I don't think you know what the problem really is.*	*That may be so, but I believe I have a right to express my feelings.* Recognize the person's feelings, but disagree that you must hold the same feelings or perceptions.

Common Detours	Your Response
Malingering: *I have such a terrible headache. I just can't think right now.*	*I'm sorry, but this is so important to me, I want to continue our talk.* Show care and concern, but insist the issue be resolved.

By following these guidelines, you are taking control of your message, as well as showing respect and concern for the relationship. You are giving helpful feedback to the person by expressing your feelings without anger. He or she may not thank you or even indicate he or she cares about what you have said. However, your release of negative feelings frees you to use your emotional energy for more positive things.

The Basic Tenets of an Assertive Philosophy

1. By standing up for our rights, we show that we respect ourselves and we achieve respect from other people.

2. By trying to govern our lives so as never to hurt anyone, we end up hurting ourselves and other people.

3. Sacrificing our rights usually results in destroying relationships or preventing new ones from forming.

4. Not letting others know how we feel and what we think is a form of selfishness.

5. Sacrificing our rights usually results in training other people to mistreat us.

6. If we don't tell other people how their behavior negatively affects us, we are denying them an opportunity to change their behavior.

7. We can decide what's important to us; we do not have to suffer from the "tyranny of the should and should not."

8. When we do what we think is right for us, we feel better about ourselves and have more authentic and satisfying relationships with others.

9. We all have a natural right to courtesy and respect.

10. We all have a right to express ourselves as long as we don't violate the rights of others.

11. There is more to be gained from life by being free and able to stand up for ourselves and from honoring the same rights of other people.

12. When we are assertive everyone involved usually benefits.

From P. Jakubowski-Spector, "Self-Assertive Training Procedures for Women." In D. Carter and E. Rawlings (Eds.), *Psychotherapy for Women: Treatment toward Equality* (Springfield, IL: Thomas, 1977).

Confidentiality and Decision Making

Leader's Goals
1. To review and expand upon the concept of confidentiality
2. To help students understand what is needed to help someone effectively
3. To differentiate between advice giving and helping
4. To introduce decision making and how to identify the important information needed to make decisions

Students' Skill Development
1. Learning how to be trustworthy
2. Identifying the information important for decision making
3. Taking charge of their own decisions

Leader's Tasks
1. To return thought cards with your comments, collect thought cards, and distribute blank thought cards
2. To discuss the transition from learning social skills to the use of these skills in specific peer-helping tasks
3. To discuss confidentiality and trust
4. To teach the decision agent activity and lead discussion concerning its application in peer helping

Materials Needed
1. Slips of paper
2. Hat, box, or paper bag
3. Flip chart and easel
4. Sheets of paper for decision agent activity
5. Cards for thought card activity

Homework Review
Ask the student leader to begin the discussion of group members' experiences talking to friends, family members, or coworkers about sensitive issues. How did people react? How did group members feel after bringing up the issue? How could they improve on practicing this skill in the future? Suggest that the students write feelings about this on their thought cards for the next session.

The student leader should choose someone to guide the homework review for the next session.

SUMMARY OF THE PREVIOUS SESSION AND TRANSITION TO THE NEXT TWO SESSIONS

In the preceding session, students worked on a skill that can benefit someone with whom they have a caring relationship. Talking to someone about a sensitive issue gives feedback that improves relationships and helps the other person develop her or his interpersonal competence. If the students have not yet talked to their chosen person about a sensitive issue, encourage them to think about why they have not done so. To give them courage to act, reinforce the idea that not handling sensitive issues is the same as denying another person help.

Up to this point in the training, group members have been learning and practicing interpersonal skills that equip them to be peer helpers in their daily lives. Ask them to name the skills that have been covered and to say which skills have been most important to them and why.

Summarize the following information for students so that they know why they are learning this session's skills.

Now group members are going to learn how to use these skills to help peers work through problems that they might bring to students or that students are asked to help solve in peer mediation. Peers who have seen the students using their new skills may see the students as trustworthy and helpful and be drawn to them. Students now need an understanding of what is involved in helping someone else work through a problem. Even though they have the desire and willingness to help, it is an awesome responsibility. No one has answers to everyone's problems, and a student's solution may not be right for another person. A "quick fix" may be useless or even make the situation worse. A peer helper who is impatient or wants quick results may lose the relationship he or she is trying to build and may create more pain for the other person. Receiving advice may make the other person feel even more helpless. For these reasons, the next two sessions are critical for group members to understand their roles as peer helpers.

CONFIDENTIALITY AND TRUST

To begin the discussion on confidentiality and trust, ask the following questions:
1. Who would you go to if you had problems with your parents?
2. Who would you go to if you had problems with a boyfriend or girlfriend?
3. Who would you turn to if you felt depressed or lonely?
4. Who would you want to talk to if a parent died or a friend committed suicide?
5. What is it about these people that would cause you to turn to them?

6. What kind of help have you received from any of these people?
7. What wasn't helpful when you turned to them?
8. What kind of help have you given to your friends when they have turned to you?
9. How confident are you about helping a friend with a problem?

Summarize group members' responses, focusing on the reasons why they would turn to particular people. Emphasize the qualities these people seem to have, what was helpful, and what wasn't. Acknowledge the students' desires to become more effective in helping friends with problems.

If students have not mentioned trust as a quality of the person they would go to, introduce this topic. If it has been mentioned, ask for their definition of trust as well as the qualities a person needs in order to be trusted. Trust is built when someone shares something personal and the information is held in confidence, meaning that this information is not revealed to anyone, not even to parents. When someone gives us the "gift" of entrusting us with personal information, it is our responsibility to keep the information confidential. On the other hand, some life-threatening issues *require* that we *not* keep a confidence (such as finding out that someone is planning to commit suicide); subjects students need to share with an adult will be covered in the next session.

EXPERIENCING LEVELS OF TRUST

Distribute a slip of paper to each person. Tell group members to write down a secret they have never shared with anyone else, or at the least, have told only one other person. The secret can be a thought or action. It may be about their family or a relationship—maybe it's a secret crush a student would rather not announce. If someone asks if group members will have to share their secrets, say that you will answer that question in a minute. Make sure students see you writing a secret, too. Give them time to think. Collect the slips in a hat, small box, or paper bag, assuring group members their secrets will remain confidential. Then discuss the activity.

1. Do you think the material in the hat [box, paper bag] could make interesting reading? (Mention that our society seems to love secrets. Lots of magazines and talk shows thrive on the revelation of other people's secrets.)
2. What would happen to this group if you selected a secret and read it aloud?
3. Tell students to look around at the people in the group. Have them think about what they would need from the group to make them willing to share their secret. List their responses on the flip chart. The key word should be *trust*. How can you build trust with others? Some group members may indicate that nothing would make them want to let others know what they wrote. Record these answers, too.

Explain that the qualities you listed are ones the students need to be a peer helper.

Trusting another person to handle personal information confidentially is essential in a helping relationship. This trust is different from having a secret between friends. As peer helpers, they must keep private almost everything that is shared, no matter how seemingly insignificant. Let each person demonstrate her or his desire to be trustworthy by passing the container around the group. Ask each person to hold it for a few seconds before passing it on.

After the hat or box or bag has been passed, shred the slips of paper. **It is extremely important that the group see you destroy the papers.**

Processing the Activity
1. What do you observe about the list on the chart?
2. What themes run through the list?
3. How does a person acquire these qualities or skills?
4. Note comments that were said about never being able to share the secret. What does this say about a person's trust in people? about the group? about the seriousness of the secret? about the person's past experience in trusting other people with personal matters?
5. Why does one person feel he or she must keep an experience or thought secret, while another with the same experience may quickly disclose the matter?
6. What value is there in sharing a secret of your own with someone?

Points to Make
1. If a person cannot trust *anyone* with personal information, it may mean that person has never experienced being trusted. This may affect others' willingness to trust this person. We have to know how to trust to be trustworthy.
2. This activity identifies the qualities and characteristics that a peer helper needs. The most common words and phrases shared are *trust, confidentiality, acceptance, understanding, a similar experience,* and *caring.* During the discussion, ask the group to add to this list, suggesting words and phrases such as *warmth, respect, personal regard, good listener,* and *nonjudgmental.* But emphasize that no one will share a real concern with a person they feel can't be *trusted.*
3. Point out that most of the words and phrases on the list represent qualities or attitudes rather than specific learned skills. Talk about how one acquires these attributes. Refer to the lesson on peer pressure and the statement, "We become who we are by the choices we make under pressure." In what other ways do we become the person we want to be?
4. In relationships, the inability to trust people is an increasing problem. A discussion on our tendency not to trust people would be useful.
5. Trust takes time to establish, but once it is broken, it can be very difficult to reestablish. Therefore, one of the key tasks students have is to responsibly handle information, even when it comes from casual conversations.

DECISION AGENT ACTIVITY

Make the transition to the purpose and function of decision making by asking the group to consider questions such as the following:

1. What do you think you will be doing when you help others make decisions?
2. What is your definition of counseling?
3. What is the difference between counseling and giving advice?
4. Why might it be harder to help others make a decision, rather than to give them advice?
5. How do you feel when someone gives you advice?

You are asking the group to participate in a type of fantasy. However, the more seriously group members take this exercise, the more they will learn from it. Use the suggested script to conduct the activity.

We often go to experts *(for example, guidance counselors, personal trainers, dieticians) to ask for advice and suggestions about aspects of our lives. When we approach an expert, we usually say what we want to happen, how much we can spend, what we don't want to do, and any other necessary information.*

We're going to focus on a new kind of expert, one who is skilled in decision making. This person is neither clairvoyant nor divine. However, this expert does have great skill in gathering information, projecting consequences, and creating legitimate options to meet our needs and goals. As long as this agent knows what someone wants and values, he or she can predict the best alternative for that person. **The decision agent is always interested in our welfare and wants to help us.**

Because of these qualifications, the agent is always in demand and has only enough time to make three decisions for any one individual. Assume you *must give three personal life decisions to this agent—decisions that you currently face or might face in the future. What would you choose? You are not just asking for information. You are turning these decisions over to the agent to make for you, and you will do what the agent decides.*

Because the agent cannot make a decision affecting your welfare without knowing certain information about you, such as what you hope to get from these decisions, you must talk to the agent. Write on a sheet of paper what you would say to the agent. Include these items:

* *The three decisions you will give away to the agent; and*
* *The information the agent will need to make these decisions in your best interest.*

Allow about 15 minutes for group members to do this. The more they think about decisions and values, the more they get from the exercise. Some may write nothing. Don't be disturbed; you can use these reactions to help teach the purpose of this exercise.

When most have finished, tell group members:

Because it worked out so well to have the agent make these decisions for you, a law has been passed **requiring that all your personal decisions be turned over to the agent, with the exception of three.** *If you could keep just three of your life decisions, which would they be? Choices can include decisions you have made in the past. Write down the three* specific *decisions you want to keep. For example, saying you want to determine your own lifestyle is too broad because it covers many personal decisions. Try to pinpoint* specific *decisions you really want to make for yourself, such as what you will do to earn a living.*

Processing the Activity

After sufficient time, write on the flip chart **Give Away** and **Keep**. Lead a discussion based on the questions below. As group members suggest examples of decisions they would give away and keep, record them on the flip chart for use in the discussion. Be prepared to share your own examples of decisions in both categories.

1. Which category was the hardest to complete? Why?
2. What are some examples of decisions you would give away?
3. What are some examples of decisions you would keep?
4. What are the differences between the kinds of decisions people would give away and those they would keep?
5. What factors might determine these differences?

Points to Make

1. Often, many students do not want to give away *any* decisions. Really push for reasons why a person wouldn't want to give away decisions. Be prepared for angry or strong emotions and appreciate these feelings when they surface. The more emotion, the more the student is experiencing the importance of the exercise. Helping others come to a decision is a delicate matter. Through this exercise, students often learn that they don't want to relinquish decisions. This realization helps them understand that others may not want to give up decisions.
2. Some young people may want to give away major decisions, such as whom to marry or what career to pursue. Never judge or act surprised when this happens—after all, these can be very difficult decisions. Our society has many different cultural norms. Acknowledge these choices later in the discussion, and remind the group to honor what another shares. People have a variety of reasons for their choices.
3. A few students may *want* to give away decisions because they don't know what they want or don't know how to make decisions. Encouraging them to list information to provide the agent helps these students identify what is important to them.
4. By deciding which decisions to keep, group members are doing the most difficult task in decision making—clarification of values. If they take it seriously, students find this the hardest category to complete.
5. Decisions people choose to give away often have short-term or less

important consequences that do not alter lives dramatically. Examples might be what to eat for dinner, what color of car to drive, or whether to wear glasses or contact lenses. However, decisions people keep usually relate to high-priority values that significantly affect quality of life, such as choice of marriage partner, friends, or religious faith.

6. We only have 24 hours per day; how we spend that time determines our quality of life. Making good decisions requires time and effort, and we simply do not have enough time to make all our decisions well. It is important, therefore, to know what we value and which decisions we do want to control so that we can devote our time to these decisions.

7. In choosing which decisions to give away, the matter of trust again emerges. We need to trust those to whom we surrender our decisions. Some students may not want to give away decisions to the agent because they lack trust in this person, despite being told that he or she was interested in their welfare.

8. We maintain some control of the decisions we give away by supplying the agent with critical information. You can give away medical decisions, for example, if you select your agent, such as a doctor, carefully and know and share your values and personal goals.

9. In reality, none of us want others to make our decisions for us. But the people we look to for help, such as parents, teachers, pastors, and friends, sometimes give advice that can affect our decisions. When people with problems approach others, they are vulnerable to surrendering their decisions, especially if they value or trust the persons to whom they turn.

   Many people come to peer helpers for a decision. However, an effective peer helper does not give advice and make someone else's choices. Instead, he or she helps a person to look at consequences and explore alternatives; the person with the problem then makes the final decision.

10. Use a quote from *Alice's Adventures in Wonderland* to make this point: When Alice was wandering in Wonderland, she came to a crossroads where she met the Cheshire Cat. "Would you tell me, please, which way I ought to go from here?" Alice asked. The Cat replied, "That depends a good deal on where you want to get to." "I don't much care where," said Alice. "Then it doesn't matter which way you go," said the Cat.

    Telling someone which path to take is giving advice. As peer helpers, the students' task is not to tell another person which way to go, thereby taking away her or his decision. Rather, their task is to help a peer determine where he or she wants to go, and then to explore the paths that will lead to that goal. How to do this will be covered in the next session.

REFLECTING ON ASSETS

Ask students to talk about assets in relation to confidentiality and trust. What assets do peer helpers demonstrate by keeping a person's secret confidential?

Mention to group members that teaching others to trust them opens the door for the people they help to trust others. This is asset building. Accepting the responsibility of being someone who can be trusted may encourage other people to risk putting trust not only in them but also in others. We all feel safer and more secure with someone we trust. Being a trustworthy role model helps others build the asset of responsibility as well.

Point out that two of the assets students are trying to build are responsibility and planning and decision making. The decision agent activity helps them learn to take responsibility for their decisions and learn how to make decisions. If group members learn to do these things now, their future lives will be enriched.

HOMEWORK ASSIGNMENT

1. Suggest that group members reflect on this lesson as they write their thought cards to be turned in at the next session.
2. Ask students to think about a current decision that they are facing or a problem they may be dealing with to bring to the next session. Let them know that you will also want them to be prepared to state the possible options and consequences for each.

Notes for Leaders

1. Some students may take the decision agent activity seriously and think there is someone who will make their decisions for them. Emphasize at the beginning that this is a fantasy.

2. You may be surprised by what you learn about your group from the decision agent exercise. You may discover group members' current concerns and insecurities about the future. Others may struggle to identify important information for the agent. Don't be dismayed if this happens. Having trouble identifying values can help students reflect on this topic, and hearing from others may lead students to self-awareness. Frustration is what you want; it often occurs when we are building self-awareness. Believe in your group members' ability to process their wants and values after the session, and encourage students to share them the next time you meet.

3. If many students find it difficult to choose which decisions to keep in the decision agent activity, consider having the group work with Handout 17, Ranking of Values. Spend time talking about the different reasons group members have for choosing their top-ranked value, as well as others on the list. This discussion exposes students to other people's values. Ask students to share how another person would know which values they hold. Do students demonstrate their values by what they do, or just by what they say? If time permits, each of the values can be discussed in some depth.

Ranking of Values

Following is a list of items you might consider important. Rank these items from 1 to 11, 1 being the most important and 11 being the least important. Try to rank what is really important to you, not what other people tell you may be important.

_____ Having one or several good friends

_____ Having spending money to go to movies, buy lunches, and other small things

_____ Getting high grades

_____ Having a boyfriend or girlfriend

_____ Having lots of free time for creative activities

_____ Living in a home with lots of comforts

_____ Devoting time to spiritual and/or personal growth

_____ Being a good athlete

_____ Learning many new things (both skills and information)

_____ Being helpful to your friends and family

_____ Being honest in your life, with family and friends, and about schoolwork

Decision Making as a Process

Leader's Goals
1. To help students understand the skills necessary to use the decision-making model
2. To demonstrate how to apply the decision-making model to personal decisions

Students' Skill Development
1. Helping others gather information relevant to decisions
2. Helping others generate possible consequences of decisions
3. Helping others evaluate alternative options

Leader's Tasks
1. To return thought cards with your comments, collect thought cards, and distribute blank thought cards
2. To teach the decision-making model
3. To demonstrate the model using a personal decision
4. To review ethical limitations and boundaries
5. To review emotional, legal, and referral issues

Materials Needed
1. A sheet of paper for each group member
2. A copy of the following for each group member:
   • Handout 18, Decision-Making Model
   • Handout 19, Ethical Limitations and Boundaries
   • Handout 20, Emotional, Legal, and Referral Issues
3. Cards for thought card activity

Homework Review

Ask the student leader to discuss thoughts or understandings the group gained from the preceding session on confidentiality and decision making. What occasions have students had in which to practice confidentiality? How did the session help them become aware of important decisions they face or are making? What questions or thoughts do they still have about critical information needed to make decisions?

The student leader should appoint someone to conduct the homework review for the next session.

SUMMARY OF THE PREVIOUS SESSION AND PURPOSE OF THIS SESSION

1. What is the most important peer-helping concept you learned from the last session?
2. What did you learn about peer helping from the *Alice's Adventures in Wonderland* quote?
3. What part of the decision-making process is hardest for you in making your own decisions?

Explain to students that in this session, they will be experiencing and learning a model they can use to help others make decisions. Whenever a peer comes to them for help, there may be emotional and legal issues that arise, whether within the relationship or because of the problem to be discussed. Group members will discuss these issues and receive guidelines for handling these situations when they arise.

INTRODUCING THE DECISION-MAKING MODEL

Hand out paper for group members to write the decision situation they were asked to prepare for this session. Have students include their name and information relevant to this decision, such as level of importance, options considered, and possible consequences.

Possible choices affect the decision-making process. Some decisions involve specific choices—either this option or that one. Many decisions, however, involve open-ended options. Some group members may have identified or considered these types of decisions. Other decisions may involve unknown factors. Decision making is difficult because we must choose one option over others that may still seem desirable or choose among multiple options that *don't* seem desirable. The task is especially difficult if students don't have any criteria for choosing from among the options. Often, the difficulty lies in the fear of the unknown consequences of our final choice. Many people do not consider the consequences of choosing to do nothing. But not deciding is also a decision.

Although helping someone through a personal problem is rarely a simple step-by-step process, there are steps to follow for guidance when working through a tough issue. The decision-making model on Handout 18 suggests a framework to follow. Each of the steps requires varying amounts of time, depending on the kind of problem and the individual with whom students are working. Group members should not attempt to move on to the next step until they are sure they have completed the preceding ones, especially the first step of identifying the real problem.

Distribute Handout 18 to the group. Discuss each step named there, giving examples to illustrate what each involves.

108

The questions listed in the decision-making model are ones you can use to explain the steps in the process. Not all would apply to every decision, and you may think of other questions that would flesh out the steps and help the group understand the model. Explain that as peer helpers, they do not need to know what action or choice the other person will take. It is only their job to help her or him through the process.

The final step of evaluating options is difficult; it means making a choice that involves a conflict of values. Direct group members' attention to the grids at step 5 and indicate that these can help them sort out choices.

State that in the spaces a person writes all the gains and losses he or she can think of related to her- or himself and others for a specific option. This process takes time, but it helps define values and provides a more objective view of the decision at hand. Any option that leads to an unacceptable loss for self or others should immediately be crossed off, unless the person is still willing to consider this option. Then the person prioritizes the gains and losses listed. Do the gains outweigh the losses? If so, this is an option to be considered seriously. The person continues working through this process with other options he or she has identified.

As leader, use a personal decision to demonstrate the decision-making model, including your evaluation of options. You will need to prepare a handout or flip-chart sheet in advance for this purpose.

Practicing Using the Model
Ask for a student to volunteer her or his decision for a demonstration. With you acting as the peer helper, proceed through this student's decision. You will not have time for a thorough look at the decision, but there will be enough time to help the group understand the process. Thank the student, and ask for her or his feelings about the process. How did it help? What did he or she learn from this process? Ask for any questions from the group.

Divide group members into pairs. Taking turns, have a partner attempt to go through the model exploring the decision the other is facing. After sufficient time, have them switch, with the other partner acting as the helper. Acknowledge that there will not be time to explore all steps in depth, but students should try to touch on each of them during the time.

Processing the Activity
1. Which step was the most challenging?
2. Do you feel you were dealing with the real problem?
3. What information seemed the most important?
4. What new options were discussed?
5. What kinds of consequences did you discuss?
6. How helpful was the process?
7. How adequate did you feel in helping your partner?
8. If you thought you couldn't help, where might your partner go for help?

9. How many of you slipped into giving advice in an effort to help? How was this advice received?

ETHICAL AND LEGAL ISSUES

Getting involved with another person's personal issues is part of a privileged relationship that involves a great deal of responsibility. It is critical that students know their boundaries. Both parties can be deeply hurt if the peer helper is not aware of the need to take certain precautions.

Occasionally, peers turn to peer helpers just for attention or friendship; they are not seeking real help. Being asked for help is flattering, and we can lose objectivity about a relationship when our egos are involved. If the person seeking help does not respond in any way to change or to work through the problem, he or she may not really want to be helped. In such cases, this issue should be addressed, and the person should be referred to someone else or be told the peer helper can no longer work with her or him.

On the other hand, students do share serious problems with peer helpers. Sometimes these problems are so urgent that a peer helper must not keep this sensitive information to her- or himself. When difficult issues arise, peer helpers can be a significant bridge between a troubled peer and the proper professional. Topics such as suicide, physical or sexual abuse, drug addictions, and mental illnesses are not in the scope of a young person's expertise to handle.

Because a peer helper is often the first to know of serious problems among her or his classmates, it is critical to discuss limitations and boundaries as well as emotional, legal, and referral issues at the conclusion of this lesson. Distribute and carefully review with students Handout 19, Ethical Limitations and Boundaries, and Handout 20, Emotional, Legal, and Referral Issues.

During this discussion, cover resources in the school and community that can provide professional help, as well as how to make a referral. Specifically discuss to whom group members should go for guidance if they are concerned about someone with whom they are working. Peer helpers need ongoing supervision as they take on the task of helping students one-on-one. Providing supervision also helps flag when someone needs help or the peer helper is confused or feeling overwhelmed by what to do.

REFLECTING ON ASSETS

Ask students which assets would be helpful to have when leading someone through a decision-making process. Responses you might hear include personal power, planning and decision making, honesty, responsibility, interpersonal competence, and positive peer influence.

HOMEWORK ASSIGNMENT

1. How a person spends her or his time is a daily decision-making process. What a person decides to do is one expression of values. Ask group members to keep track of how they spend their time during the next week. Have them record in their journals at the end of each day what they did in their unscheduled time, particularly after school or in the evening. Tell them to bring these records to the next session.

2. Remind students to bring in their thought cards or to email you.

Notes for Leaders

1. You do not know what kind of a problem or decision you will be working with when you demonstrate the decision-making model. Your time will be limited, so concentrate on identifying the problem, which really is the model's hardest step. Clarifying the real problem may help the person decide which path to take. Often, people are confused about what is bothering them. An objective helper using open-ended, nonjudgmental questioning and listening can lead the person to the problem's source. If revealing the true problem is all you can cover, talk through where you would go with this problem if there were more time.

2. The person whose decision has been used in the demonstration can still participate in the pairing. Her or his partner can continue to work through the problem with which you started.

3. Make sure you are completely knowledgeable about the model, and practice using it with at least one of your own decisions.

4. Group members need to know that because they are dealing with a legal minor, they should never make a referral without consulting their peer-helping adviser. To guide your group members appropriately, you will need to research and become familiar with your state's [province's] laws regarding referrals for legal minors.

5. Make your training environment as asset-rich as possible. Reread the material in the sidebar on pages xiv–xv in the introduction to be sure you are acting as an asset role model.

Decision-Making Model

STEP

1. Identify the Problem

Ask: What are you trying to decide?

Why do you need to make this decision?

Who is involved?

What is involved?

What options are available to you?

What seems to keep you from
making the decision?

2. Explore Values

Ask: Why is this important to you?

What do you want to have happen?

How will you gain from this decision?

How might you lose or suffer as a result
of this decision?

How might someone else suffer as a result
of this decision?

Are there any possible consequences you
couldn't live with?

How much are you willing to risk to get
what you want?

3. Examine Past Solutions

Ask: What have you already tried?

What choices have you already considered?

What past experiences might help you
in this decision?

4. Examine Present Options

Ask: What other possible options might you
consider?

What obstacles might you encounter with
these options?

What might be the consequences of any
of these options?

Who might be hurt by any of these choices?

QUESTION

What is the problem?

What do you want?

What have you already tried?

What are your current options?

112

STEP
5. Evaluate Your Options

QUESTION
What will you gain or lose?

Option 1:

	GAINS	LOSSES
SELF		
OTHERS		

Option 2:

	GAINS	LOSSES
SELF		
OTHERS		

Decision Making as a Process

Ethical Limitations and Boundaries

Various critical factors come into play when you offer to help a person deal with a problem. Ethics are a set of moral principles or values.

- The person with the problem is *vulnerable.* Suggestions, advice, even kindness and caring take on a heightened meaning.

- As the one to whom the person has turned for help, you have a lot of *power* to influence this person. Power results from information entrusted to you, as well as the revelation of weaknesses and emotions normally kept private. You have a responsibility to be careful and ethical with this power.

- Your *motives* must be caring. You must be focused on the person's welfare and safety. Using another person to feel needed or to get recognition for yourself is unethical.

- The *methods* you use to help must fit with your training and ability level. Trying to help someone with an issue that is too much for you to handle can present potential danger or emotional harm to the person.

- A peer helper does not have the credentials of a professional counselor. Situations beyond your range of experience or training must be referred to those with appropriate expertise. Your critical task may be to serve as a *bridge* between the person seeking or needing help and the proper professional resource. If someone keeps returning to you as a peer helper to talk about the same problem, it is most likely time to refer the person to a professional counselor.

- As a peer helper, you cannot guarantee that *everything* will be held in confidence. You may need to state something like, "If you're about to hurt yourself or someone else, I'll need to tell an adult to get you the proper help."

Emotional, Legal, and Referral Issues

Emotional Issues

Never date someone you are trying to help as a way of relating to her or him. A relationship of this nature would compromise your role as a peer helper and could possibly lead to emotional problems for both you and the helpee (the person who has come to you for help).

Be sensitive to emotional attachments that might develop between your helpee and you. Even though you may be flattered, forming a romantic relationship with a peer you are trying to help is not ethical. Be direct about the boundaries and purposes of the relationship. Only under completely different circumstances might a romantic relationship be appropriate. Anytime you are getting involved emotionally, evaluate your need. Emotional attachment distorts your ability to be objective and may only add to the person's problem. Under these circumstances, it may be prudent to refer the person to another peer helper.

Legal Issues

By law, the following situations are outside the bounds of confidentiality and must be reported:
- Sexual or physical abuse
- Possession of illegal weapons or declaration of intent to harm self or others
- Illegal activity of any kind

When you encounter such issues working with someone, by law you are required to report the situation to someone in authority, such as a school counselor, principal, or police officer. If you anticipate that any of these issues may be involved or mentioned, inform the person or group—before such information is revealed. (See the last item on Handout 19 for help.)

Referral Issues
- Always be ready with people and resources to contact when you are concerned about another or your ability to help. You may feel it will be a bother or that it is not

right to contact someone; but a peer group leader or your school counselor is always available for help, and they want you to call—it is *their* job to help *you.*

- Those who talk of personally destructive behavior, including suicide and drug use, or who have delusional plans (which could indicate psychological disturbance) must get professional care. You cannot help in these situations, other than by getting the person professional help.

- In dealing with a legal minor, never make a referral without consulting with your peer-helping adviser or school counselor.

Conflict Mediation Skills—Part 1

Leader's Goals
1. To demonstrate how assumptions and differing perceptions affect interpersonal relationships
2. To help students understand how new information can change perceptions and judgmental assumptions

Students' Skill Development
1. Gaining awareness of filters that can result in conflict and/or affect behavior in conflicts
2. Reducing conflict by suspending judgment of self and others
3. Identifying factors that trigger assumptions about others
4. Expressing emotions in nonaggressive, noninflammatory ways

Leader's Tasks
1. To return thought cards with your comments, collect thought cards, and distribute blank thought cards
2. To invite a visitor to meet with the group
3. To prepare a list of group members with space for writing

Materials Needed
1. Flip chart and easel
2. List of questions for visitor to ask
3. Paper for writing personal perceptions
4. Copies of list of group members
5. Cards for thought card activity

Homework Review

Have the student leader ask for reports on how the students spent their time in the past week. Where did they spend the majority of their free time? What did they neglect in their use of time? What consequences resulted from these choices? What did this activity reveal about their values?

The student leader should select someone to guide the homework review for the next session.

SUMMARY OF THE PREVIOUS SESSION AND PURPOSE OF THIS SESSION

Ask someone to review the steps in the decision-making model. Write down steps on the flip chart as they are mentioned. Ask the students if they can remember some of the questions to ask for each of the steps. When they are finished, add those questions that were missed.

Ask: What was most useful about this model? In what experiences, if any, did you have a chance to use the model during the past week?

Summarize the following information for students to put this session into context:

This session and the following one focus on the skills of conflict mediation. The previous sessions covered interpersonal skills for building one-on-one, peer-helping relationships, but these very same skills of questioning, listening for feelings, handling sensitive issues, and decision making are the ones needed to be an effective peer mediator. However, additional skills and aptitudes are needed for this specialized task, such as perceptual abilities and being able to control one's emotional responses when conflicts arise and are discussed. When learned, such skills will serve youth long into the future in interpersonal relationships, and peer helpers can teach these skills to their peers.

This session will focus on perceptual and emotional abilities. The next session will focus on the peer mediation process and the practice of related skills.

EXPERIENCE WITH CONFLICTS

Ask how many of the group members know about peer mediation or have been peer mediators. If some group members have learned this process through other activities, acknowledge that you will use them to teach this skill to the others in the group.

Begin the discussion by asking:
1. When you think of conflict, what words come to mind?
2. Which of those words are negative?
3. Which words are positive?
4. How might conflict be positive?
5. What kind of conflicts do you see going on around the world today?
6. What are these about?
7. How are these conflicts being dealt with?
8. How successfully are they being resolved?
9. What do you think is needed to resolve these conflicts?
10. What are your emotional reactions to these conflicts?
11. How do these conflicts affect your daily lives?

As students share, highlight on the flip chart the issues, feelings, and ideas for resolution that they mention. Continue the discussion by asking the following questions:

1. What kinds of family conflicts do you experience?
2. What are these usually about?
3. With whom do they usually occur?
4. Who starts it?
5. Why do you think the other person does what he or she does?
6. How do you react?
7. What do you regret, if anything, after the conflict is over?
8. What possible motives might the person have other than the one(s) you accuse her or him of?
9. How could these matters be settled differently?

Add to the flip chart list additional issues, emotions, motives, and resolution ideas.

Now ask what kinds of conflicts group members have or have had with their peers. Ask the same questions you asked about family conflicts. Add any new thoughts to the list you have started.

Have students study the items on the chart to see what common threads have emerged from conflicts they have described. Ask: What common issues are at stake? What are common assumptions, feelings, responses, and results?

Using these themes, explain that conflicts center on basic needs that everyone has, as described in William Glasser's control theory. We have the need of *belonging,* which means being loved, as well as sharing and cooperating with others. We have the need for *power,* realized by achieving and accomplishing, as well as being recognized and respected. We also need *freedom* to make choices in our lives and to feel safe. And we need *fun* through laughter and play. Whenever any of these needs are not met, or another person gets in the way of our fulfilling these needs, we tend to fight for them, forgetting that the other person has the same needs and is also trying to fulfill them. Illustrate these points by using examples group members shared during the conflict discussion. Suggest that students think about how these needs are met for them when they fill out their next thought card.

PERCEPTUAL SKILLS: THE VISITOR INTERVIEW

Often conflicts are accelerated by misunderstandings, assumptions, and perceived negative motives. When we learn to control our emotions, calm ourselves, and review our assumptions, conflicts can be kept from spinning out of control. Then possible positive solutions can be reached in which both parties win. To do this, we have to become aware of the filters we use to judge others. Becoming aware of these filters is often hard to do.

Tell the group that in just a few moments, you will welcome a visitor who will ask the group questions about her- or himself. Group members will be asked to answer these questions based on their observations of the visitor. Even though students' observations may not seem complimentary, they should answer the questions honestly. The visitor is prepared for group members' possible answers.

Select a person the students do not know to be the visitor. This person should be someone whose dress, appearance, race, ethnicity, or disability may mask the real person he or she is. For example, students may be surprised to find out that a person who uses a wheelchair is an athlete. Previous to the visit, prepare the visitor for what you want to demonstrate and the questions you want her or him to ask the group. Explain to the students that at the end of the visitor's questioning, he or she will answer all of the questions with facts about her- or himself. The following are suggestions of questions to ask, but you can add others as appropriate:

1. What kind of work do you think I do?
2. How much education do I have?
3. What kind of car do I drive?
4. What do I like to do for fun?
5. In what kind of activities do I participate within the community?
6. What was I like as a teenager (if an adult)?
7. What kind of sports do I enjoy watching?
8. What are my images of teenagers?
9. Whom do I admire?
10. What do I do when I have an argument with someone?
11. What do you like about me?

When finished getting student responses, have the guest answer the same questions briefly. Then ask for her or his reactions to this experience and perceptions of the students.

Processing the Experience

1. What surprised you when you learned the real facts about our guest?
2. What was there about the person that triggered your answers to her or his questions?
3. What answers did you want to give but were too embarrassed to say when the visitor was here?
4. How did your perceptions change after you learned the true answers to questions?
5. What did you learn about the filters you have in judging this person?
6. How have these filters affected your judgment of classmates, adults, strangers?
7. How could you apply what you learned from this activity to your daily lives?

PERCEPTIONS OF GROUP MEMBERS

Give everyone a piece of paper. Ask group members to write their perceptions of themselves. Have them consider every aspect about themselves: appearance, physical attributes, abilities, personalities, and others' perceptions of them. Urge students to think of the **positive** perceptions they have as well as the possible negatives. They should not be worried about spelling or sentence structure. They should just let their minds wander freely and honestly. Allow 10–15 minutes for this writing. Have the students sign their papers when finished. Then collect them.

Next pass out a sheet with the names of all group members and space between the names for them to write. Ask them to now write positive perceptions they have of each person on the list, excluding themselves. Allow 10–15 minutes for this activity. Then, ask the group to sign the sheets and turn them in.

Processing the Activity
1. How did you feel about thinking of positive perceptions of others?
2. What new observations did you make about others in the group?
3. How often have you expressed these perceptions to others? If not, why not?
4. How might this activity change how you treat one another?
5. How might this activity help you to listen to or understand one another in a new way?
6. What effect did putting your perceptions in writing have on seeing others in a positive light?

SHARING PERCEPTIONS

It is one thing to write perceptions and another to express them verbally, especially when they are negative. However, it is our negative perceptions that often trigger conflicts. Practice in sharing perceptions can help us gain the ability to empathize with others; see other interpretations of what has been said or done; and/or possibly reframe what has been said or done in a way that preserves the dignity of the other person and shows respect.

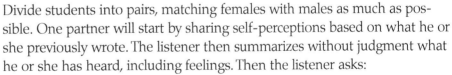

Divide students into pairs, matching females with males as much as possible. One partner will start by sharing self-perceptions based on what he or she previously wrote. The listener then summarizes without judgment what he or she has heard, including feelings. Then the listener asks:
1. How do you think your self-perceptions might contribute to conflicts?
2. How do you think these perceptions affect your responses to conflict?
3. How do you think your perceptions help avoid conflicts?

No interpretations of the answers to the questions are needed. Then the listener shares her or his positive perceptions of the speaker.

Repeat the exercise with the first listener sharing personal perceptions and the other person acting as the listener.

Processing the Activity
1. What was hard about doing this activity? Why?
2. What did you learn about yourself from doing this?
3. What was easy and what was difficult if your partner was of the opposite sex?
4. What was easy and what was difficult if your partner was of the same sex?
5. What did your partner do that helped you talk about perceptions?
6. How helpful was the partner's feedback on what you said?
7. What did you learn from answering the questions asked of you?
8. What surprised you about hearing your partner's perceptions of you?
9. What different emotions are felt when you hear positive feedback about yourself?
10. How do these emotions differ from ones you experience when you get negative feedback?
11. What perceptions do you usually expect to hear from others?
12. How does the discrepancy between what you expect to hear and what you actually hear contribute to conflicts you experience?

REFLECTING ON ASSETS

Have students think back to the homework review. Talk about the assets in the constructive-use-of-time category, asset #25 (reading for pleasure), and asset #9 (service to others). These relate to how students spend their free time.

Talk about William Glasser's control theory in relation to the assets. The need of belonging relates to the assets we need in the support category. The need for power is associated with our need for positive identity and empowerment. The need for freedom and fun also relate to empowerment as well as constructive use of time.

One of the 40 developmental assets is peaceful conflict resolution. Learning to be peer mediators contributes significantly to building this asset.

HOMEWORK ASSIGNMENT
1. Ask each person to write a script of a current or recent conflict situation. These scripts should include a statement of the conflict; who the disputants are; and background information about each of the disputants that explains a little about each person's position, her or his view of the situation, and hints about needs or feelings that may contribute to the dispute. State that these scripts will be used in the next session.
2. Encourage students to identify their perceptions of family members or peers that tend to lead to conflicts. Ask them to think about the

following questions: When a family member's or peer's behavior upsets you, can you think about what possible reasons that person might have for behaving that way? What might he or she want or need from you, and how are you tempted to respond? Have the students write their observations in their journals.

3. Ask students to bring in their final list of ways to build assets for and with their peers. Tell them you will combine these lists for them to distribute throughout their school or community.

4. Remind group members to bring in or email their thought cards.

Notes for Leaders

1. The purpose of starting with conflicts in the world today is partly to show how pervasive conflicts are in our daily lives. It also helps the group realize how far conflicts may go when people do not know how to resolve them in peaceful ways. Talking about conflicts in today's world is a safe way to explore the topic of conflict while still stirring up emotions and differing opinions on how conflicts should be resolved.

2. The issue of family conflicts brings the discussion closer to home and leads into peer conflicts. The same questions asked about families can be asked about peer relationships. These questions illustrate your goals for this session.

3. The visitor's presence can demonstrate how quickly we make snap judgments about others based on physical traits, clothing, race, gender, ethnicity, or other factors. It is important that the visitor be someone whose outward appearance might trigger inaccurate perceptions. The visitor should be carefully briefed on what you are trying to demonstrate, what is expected of her or him, and possible answers he or she might get.

4. Writing self-perceptions leads to self-awareness. Often self-perceptions dictate how we behave based on our assumptions of how others see us. Self-assumptions reveal our vulnerabilities that can easily spark conflict. Honest, positive feedback from a peer can dramatically change attitudes and beliefs. For these reasons it is critical that members only give positive perceptions. Having been together for a considerable period of time, group members have had sufficient time to make positive observations.

5. The leader *must* compile all the positive perceptions from the students' lists for each person in the group. Each student will then get an account of how others see her or him. As leader, write your own positive perceptions on the self-perceptions students have turned in, and return these to the students at the next session.

6. Ask someone to write a thank-you to the visitor who came to the group that day. Tell the volunteer you will collect the letter next time to mail it.

Conflict Mediation Skills—Part 2

Leader's Goals
1. To teach the peer mediation process
2. To help students value the peer mediation process in settling conflicts

Students' Skill Development
1. Using interpersonal skills as peer mediators
2. Critiquing strengths and weaknesses as peer mediators
3. Applying the peer mediation process to personal conflicts

Leader's Tasks
1. To collect the thank-you letter for last session's visitor
2. To return thought cards with your comments, collect thought cards, and distribute blank thought cards
3. To demonstrate the peer mediation process
4. To summarize class members' perceptions of one another and write leader's perceptions of each group member for distribution
5. To collect student lists of ways to build assets for and with their peers

Materials Needed
1. Flip chart and easel
2. A copy of the following for each group member:
   - Handout 21, The Peer Mediation Process
   - Handout 22, Dos and Don'ts of Peer Mediation
   - Handout 23, Mike and Denisha Conflict Scenario
   - Handout 24, Conflict Management Report
3. Individual lists of group members' positive perceptions of one another
4. Cards for thought card activity

Homework Review

Ask the student leader to guide the discussion. How much did students question their perceptions of others throughout the week? How did the activity of talking about self-perceptions and getting feedback from a group member affect their behavior throughout the week? How did it affect potential conflicts that may have arisen in the past week? What was most helpful about the previous lesson?

SUMMARY OF THE PREVIOUS SESSION AND PURPOSE OF THIS SESSION

In the last session, we focused on perceptions of self and others. What did you learn about perceptions and physical appearance? How might perceptions be related to personal conflicts? Consider people who are different from you, perhaps in race, ethnicity, religious beliefs, or social status. How might perceptions affect your relationships with them? How do you form the perceptions you have about yourself? What keeps us from sharing positive perceptions with others? Would we experience fewer conflicts if we practiced positive feedback with our peers?

Share the following information with your group members as a guide to this session's activities.

This session will be devoted to learning and practicing the **peer mediation process.** It's possible that as peer helpers, students will be asked to act as peer mediators in conflict resolution situations. To do this, they need to understand thoroughly the mediation process and practice it in conflict situations.

Definition: Peer mediation is a voluntary method for negotiating disputes and finding resolutions that satisfy the needs of the involved parties. It is a step-by-step process led by two student mediators; however, each situation requires flexibility and spontaneity. The two peer mediators' roles are proactive—that is, their responsibility is to create and maintain an atmosphere that fosters cooperative, collaborative problem solving. Successful mediation relies upon the skills that peer helpers have learned for developing healthy interpersonal relationships and helping others to work through problems.

DEMONSTRATING THE STEPS OF MEDIATION

Distribute copies of Handout 21, The Peer Mediation Process, and Handout 22, Dos and Don'ts of Mediation. Discuss the process, covering each point slowly and carefully. When finished, explain that you will demonstrate the process using a conflict situation. Tell the group that although normally there would be two mediators, only you will act as mediator for this demonstration. Ask for two volunteers to take the roles of Mike and Denisha. Give each of them the conflict scenario and the appropriate character background information (Handout 23). Tell the students that as you demonstrate the steps, they might want to take notes for future reference. The steps are as follows:

1. Prepare before the Mediation Begins
2. Make Introductions
3. Establish Ground Rules
4. Gather Information
5. Find Common Interests
6. Brainstorm Possible Solutions

7. Make an Agreement
8. Conclude Mediation

1. **Prepare before the Mediation Begins:** As group members sit in a circle, arrange seating for the mediation in the circle's center. The chairs or desks should form a V shape with the two mediators at the peak and one disputant at the side of each mediator, facing each other.

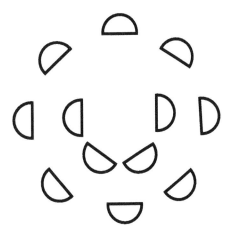

Tell students that the first step is to have pens and Conflict Management Report forms ready (Handout 24). Explain to the group that some students may be referred to peer mediation by someone else. In these cases, the mediators should review the reason for the referral. State that the next step is for them to decide on their roles—that is, which mediator will handle which steps.

2. **Make Introductions:** Bring your Mike and Denisha volunteers to the circle's center. Welcome them and introduce yourselves. Explain the process and the principles of confidentiality.

3. **Establish Ground Rules:** Review each ground rule and get verbal agreement from Denisha and Mike to abide by the rule.

4. **Gather Information:** Ask Denisha to describe what happened. Summarize Denisha's point of view, checking with her to see if your summary is correct.

Turn to Mike and ask him for his explanation of events. Summarize what Mike says, checking to see if you heard accurately.

Ask in turn for additional comments about the conflict and continue to do so until the disputants have stated all the important information. Each time Mike or Denisha offers a statement, summarize what you heard before seeking a statement from the other person. Ask questions such as: "What did you think when that happened?" "Could you explain more about that?" Tell students that while gathering points of view, the mediator also must validate each disputant's concerns and feelings as well as clarify the history and sequence of events of the conflict.

5. **Find Common Interests:** Ask Denisha and Mike, "What do you want and why do you want that?" Explain to students that the *what* is the position, and the *why* is the interest. At this point, Mike and Denisha may discover that they share certain interests or that their interests, even if different, are compatible. Ask: "What do you really want?" "If you were in the other person's shoes, how would you feel?" "What would you think?" and "What might happen if you don't reach an agreement?"

As Denisha and Mike answer these questions, summarize each person's interests. Explain to students that doing this makes common interests explicit and clarifies them as shared goals. Direct disputants to these common goals by statements such as, "Both of you seem to agree that_____."

6. **Brainstorm Possible Solutions**: Ask Mike and Denisha to brainstorm ideas that might solve this conflict. At this point, they are not rying to determine the best solution but to generate a number of ideas that might meet the interests of both. Tell them to say any ideas that come to mind and not to judge or discuss the ideas. Come up with as many ideas as possible, and try to think of unusual ones.

Tell students that the mediator can help the process by asking: "What other possibilities can you think of?" "In the future, what could you do differently?" The mediator may have to remind Mike and Denisha of the common interests they identified in step 5: "You both agreed that these were your common interests. What ideas would help them happen?" Record their ideas on the flip chart.

Ask Mike and Denisha to choose, from the list of solutions they brainstormed, the ideas or parts of ideas they think are fair and have the best possibility of working. Circle the ideas each suggests. Now Mike and Denisha must evaluate and improve upon the circled options. The mediator may ask questions such as: "Is this option fair?" "Can you do it?" "Do you think it will work?" "What are the consequences of deciding to do this?" "Does this option address the interests you have in common?"

7. **Make an Agreement:** Once Mike and Denisha have discussed the various options, ask them to make a plan of action. When they come to an agreement, help them check whether it is sound. Is it *balanced, specific, realistic, lasting,* and *fair?* Do both parties have a part to play in the resolution? Ask each person to summarize what he or she is agreeing to. If either person does not accurately state the agreement, clarify by saying, "I thought I heard you agree to_____."

Once the agreement is clear to both parties, ask them to sign a written agreement expressing their intent. If problems arise after mediation, a well-written agreement can clarify issues.

8. **Conclude Mediation:** Congratulate Mike and Denisha on caring enough about their friendship to participate in mediation and to work out a plan that will help them avoid future conflict. State that mediation may in fact strengthen their friendship.

When the demonstration is over, ask the students who played Mike and Denisha to evaluate the process and what they learned from this demonstration. Ask the group for reactions and/or questions.

PRACTICING THE MEDIATION PROCESS

Divide the students into groups of four. Tell the small groups to take the scripts they wrote as part of their homework for this session and either choose one or combine them to create a script they can use to practice the mediation process. Group members must clarify the conflict and who the disputants are. They must also give background information that describes each disputant's position and view of the situation, as well as some hints about personal needs or feelings that may be contributing to the dispute.

Explain that each group will choose another group's script to practice the mediation process. There will be two mediators. Having two mediators share responsibility for monitoring and facilitation helps assure quality in the process. The mediators work together by handling separate steps in the process. For example, one mediator may facilitate steps 2, 4, and 6 (Make Introductions, Gather Information, and Brainstorm Possible Solutions). The other may take the lead on steps 3, 5, and 7 (Establish Ground Rules, Find Common Interests, and Make an Agreement). Both can work through the final step of concluding the mediation. Once the mediation is over, the mediators can give feedback to one another.

Have the groups hand in their scripts. Then ask the first group to pick a script other than their own. Continue to have each group select a script. Give students time to study their scripts and to choose who will be the mediators and who will be the disputants. When ready, begin the practice sessions, having each group take turns.

Processing the Mediations

Process each mediation after its conclusion. Start by allowing the mediators to evaluate themselves. **Keep the focus on the mediators, not on the conflict.** Self-evaluation sustains the mediators' dignity by allowing them to identify weaknesses before others call attention to them.
Then proceed with the following questions:
1. How do the disputants feel about the process?
2. What common interests did the disputants discover?

3. How did the discovery of common interests help in reaching a solution?
4. What feelings did the mediators pick up on?
5. Were the disputants committed to the solution?
6. What did the group observe about the process?
7. What suggestions could group members give the mediators?
8. How effectively did the mediators understand the problem from both disputants' points of view?
9. How realistic was the mediation to the disputants? Explain.

Have subsequent groups practice the process with their chosen scripts. Use the same processing questions as those above. The first practice sessions may be difficult, but each group will grow from the preceding experience. Students need practice to learn the process and build confidence in their abilities.

When all groups have finished, ask for a general evaluation of what the students learned and how confident they feel in using this process. How do group members see using this in their everyday lives?

DISTRIBUTING CLASS PERCEPTIONS

Dealing with conflicts stirs up many different emotions. Because group members have been dealing with their own issues, it is important now to distribute the group members' **positive** perceptions of one another. The positive perceptions should give each person a lift. Give each person the perceptions you have compiled for her or him, along with the self-perception sheet on which you've commented. Give students time to read them. Don't ask for responses, but allow a discussion of feelings if comments are forthcoming. Often students are awed by how positively classmates view them.

REFLECTING ON ASSETS

Each step in the mediation process can help mediators build their own developmental assets. Discuss the following list of the steps and the assets they build.

Step 1. Prepare before the Mediation Begins	Planning and decision making
Step 2. Make Introductions	Interpersonal competence; cultural competence
Step 3. Establish Ground Rules	Boundaries and expectations assets
Step 4. Gather Information	Honesty; responsibility; interpersonal competence
Step 5. Find Common Interests	Caring; interpersonal competence
Step 6. Brainstorm Possible Solutions	Planning and decision making; personal power
Step 7. Make an Agreement	Responsibility; personal power

Step 8. Conclude Mediation

Youth as resources; peaceful conflict resolution

Conclude by asking students how they think the skill of mediation can help them build assets for and with their peers. Additional assets that might be brought up in the discussion include service to others, high expectations, self-esteem, and sense of purpose.

HOMEWORK ASSIGNMENT

Ask students to write their own peer-helping mission statement based on the skills they have learned and used.

Notes for Leaders

1. If you have already used this training once, consider asking two previous students to model the peer mediation process instead of demonstrating it yourself.
2. Distributing group members' personal perceptions of individual students at the end of the session is important because it leaves students with positive feelings. You may be amazed at how moved students are by these comments.
3. If you are using this training in a school setting, have school administrators decide how they want a peer mediation program to work. For example, will staff refer students to peer mediation? Will the school publicize the program so that any students having a dispute can use the program if they would like? Share the administration's desires with the students so that they know how they will be involved, where mediation will take place, and other details.
4. During the final session, you will want to recognize the group members' completion of assignments throughout the training. Most important is tabulation of the students' lists of ways to build assets for and with peers. When they bring in their lists, compile and copy them for distribution during the final session. Also, be prepared to discuss with your group how members can use these lists within their school and community.
5. Early in the training you asked students to write a peer-helping mission statement. Their understanding may have deepened as training proceeded. Having group members write their own understanding is a way of helping them evaluate what the training has meant to them.
6. It is important for group members to review the 40 assets and to reflect on how these influence their developmental growth and how they can help others experience developmental assets. Some of the final session will be devoted to this idea.

The Peer Mediation Process

1. Prepare before the Mediation Begins
A. Arrange seating in the room.
B. Have pens and Conflict Management Report forms (Handout 24) ready.
C. Review the reason for the referral if you have been told it.
D. Divide the mediator roles.

2. Make Introductions
A. Welcome disputants and congratulate them for wanting to resolve their conflict in a mature way.
B. Introduce the two conflict mediators.
C. Have each disputant introduce her- or himself.
D. Explain the process.
E. Tell the disputants that what is said in this room will stay in this room, except for mentions of child abuse, illegal activity, and threats to injure oneself or others.

3. Establish Ground Rules
Introduce the following ground rules and get verbal agreement from both disputants for each one. They must agree:
— to try to solve the problem.
— not to interrupt.
— that there will be no name-calling or put-downs.
— to be honest.
— that there will be no physical fighting.
— to speak directly to the mediators at first.

4. Gather Information
A. Ask disputant #1, "What happened?" Summarize.
   Ask disputant #1, "How does this situation make you feel and why?" Summarize.
B. Ask disputant #2, "What happened?" Summarize.
   Ask disputant #2, "How does this situation make you feel and why?" Summarize.
C. Ask disputant #1 if he or she has anything to add. Summarize.
D. Ask disputant #2 if he or she has anything to add. Summarize.
E. Ask questions and make comments that will help you as mediators understand the problem. For example, How long? How often? What do you mean? When? Tell me more about this. Summarize.

F. Summarize each disputant's position and ask her or him to verify that your summary is accurate.

5. Find Common Interests
A. Ask disputant #2, "What do you want and why do you want it?" Summarize.
B. Ask disputant #1, "What do you want and why do you want it?" Summarize.
C. Ask disputant #1, "If you were in_____'s shoes, how would you feel?" Summarize.
D. Ask disputant #2, "If you were in_____'s shoes, how would you feel?" Summarize.
E. Ask each disputant, "Is there anything else the other disputant should know about you?" Summarize.
F. When you find information that they both share, tell them what they have in common. "Both of you seem to agree that_____." (shared goals)
G. Again summarize positions of each disputant.

6. Brainstorm Possible Solutions
A. Ask each person in turn what he or she sees as possible solutions: "What do you need from ____to have this problem solved?"
B. Ask the other person if he or she heard that and have her or him restate it.
C. Ask if there is anything else or add any possible solutions you see that might resolve this issue in a positive way: "Have you thought of____?" "What about____?"

7. Make an Agreement
"What can you do so you both get what you need?"
"Is the problem solved using this solution?"
"Can you both agree to that solution?"
Make sure the solution is realistic, specific, balanced, lasting, and fair.
"What needs to happen first to make the solution work? Then what?"

8. Conclude Mediation
A. Congratulate the disputants on their work to resolve their differences.
B. Tell them to let others know that they have worked out their conflict so that rumors aren't spread.
C. Ask each disputant what he or she could do differently if this problem comes up again. Summarize.
D. Fill out a Conflict Management Report and have each disputant sign it.
E. Make a copy of the report for each disputant.
F. Encourage them to come back if they have any more problems.

Dos and Don'ts of Mediation

Do . . .

1. Listen carefully.

2. Be fair.

3. Ask how each person feels.

4. Let each person state what happened.

5. Keep what you are told confidential.

6. Treat each person with respect.

7. Mediate in private.

Don't . . .

1. Take sides.

2. Tell the disputants what to do.

3. Ask who started it.

4. Try to blame anyone for the situation.

5. Give advice.

6. Ask, "Why did you do it?"

7. Look for witnesses.

Mediation Rules for the Disputants

- Be willing to solve the problem.
- Tell the truth.
- Listen without interrupting.
- Be respectful: no name-calling, put-downs, or fighting.
- Take responsibility for carrying out your agreement.

Rule for Mediators

Remain neutral.

Mike and Denisha Conflict Scenario

Directions: Give conflict and character background information to both Denisha and Mike; however, do not give Denisha's background information to Mike, and vice versa.

Disputants: Two good friends, Mike and Denisha

Conflict: Mike and Denisha share a locker at school. Denisha is very neat and keeps her books, clothes, and gym equipment arranged carefully in her space. Mike is disorganized and impulsive. He tosses things into the locker, forgets to remove things such as old lunches, and throws in gym clothes that need to be washed. Occasionally, he borrows Denisha's books when he can't find his own in his mess. Denisha sometimes throws out Mike's lunches and papers that she doesn't think are important to him in an attempt to keep the locker neat. Yesterday she took his dirty gym clothes home to wash to stop the smell they left in the locker. The next afternoon, Mike looked for them to wear to practice. He was furious when he realized his gym clothes were gone, and he knew exactly what happened to them. He grabbed most of Denisha's books from the locker. Before Denisha went home, she stopped at her locker to get some books she needed for a test the next day. They were gone and she became frantic. Denisha called Mike that night and they had an angry exchange. They agreed to go to mediation.

Character Background (give to Denisha)
Denisha is ashamed of the locker's appearance. She often has to sift through Mike's things to find her own books and belongings. She wants to teach Mike a lesson, and she wants him to respect her things and her half of the locker. She often is angered when something is missing, and she knows that Mike has borrowed it.

Character Background (give to Mike)
Mike is more carefree. He sees the locker simply as a holding place for items while he has better things to do. Occasionally, he cleans out stuff he hasn't used or thought about for a while. Sometimes when he can't find a textbook he needs, he borrows Denisha's, thinking she won't mind, and eventually he returns it. He thinks she is too uptight about neatness and needs to loosen up.

Conflict Management Report

Date _____

We voluntarily participated in mediation. We have reached an agreement that we believe is fair and that solves the problem between us. In the future, if we have a problem that we cannot resolve on our own, we agree to come back to mediation.

Name_____   Name_____

I agree to: _____   I agree to: _____

_____   _____

_____   _____

_____   _____

_____   _____

_____   _____

_____   _____

_____   _____

_____   _____

_____   _____

Signature _____   Signature _____

Mediator's signature _____

Mediator's signature _____

Asset Building as a Life Choice

Leader's Goals
1. To review students' knowledge and understanding of the 40 developmental assets
2. To have students reflect on the benefits this training has had on their personal growth
3. To have group members evaluate the peer-helping training

Students' Skill Building
1. Expressing self-awareness of developmental growth
2. Analyzing ways to implement asset building
3. Evaluating the value of peer-helping training

Leaders' Tasks
1. To return thought cards with your comments
2. To summarize the training
3. To collect training evaluations
4. To hand out the compiled list of ways to build assets for and with the students' peers. Ask students to find creative ways to distribute this list throughout local schools and communities.
5. To have students reveal whom they observed over the course of the training

Materials Needed
1. A copy of the following for each group member:
   - Handout 25, Training Evaluation
   - Handout 26, The 40 Assets without Definitions
   - Handout 27, Identifying Assets Game
   - Handout 28, Answers for Identifying Assets
2. A blank postcard for each group member
3. Prizes, gifts, and/or certificates to distribute

Homework Review
Pass out the compiled list of ways to build assets for and with peers. Have group members read through the list. Do some ideas seem more difficult to implement than others? What makes them difficult? What might the students need to implement them? How could they help one another put

these ideas to work? How can students get their parents, school, and community involved in implementing some of these ideas?

Ask student volunteers to read the peer-helping mission statement you asked them to write. How committed are students to practicing this mission in their daily lives? What kind of support do they need to meet this commitment now that training is finished? Should the group meet again in a month to review each person's commitment?

SUMMARY OF THE PREVIOUS SESSION AND PURPOSE OF THIS SESSION

Tell the students that in the preceding session, you reviewed the steps in conflict mediation. Ask someone to go over the steps. Which steps do group members find most difficult? What are some of the dos they should remember when conducting mediation?

Because this is the final session, it is helpful to have the group reflect on what has been covered during the training and to evaluate what they feel they have learned. It is also important to enhance their knowledge and understanding of all the 40 assets. Start a review of the skills they have learned by asking students to list the skills and concepts that have been covered. Students may remember some skills readily. However, some principal concepts, such as confidentiality, personal qualities and skills demonstrated through past achievements, feelings vocabularies, observations, and exploration of thoughts and values through thought cards, may be less vivid to students. If some are not mentioned, remind the group of them.

EVALUATING THE VALUE OF PEER-HELPING TRAINING

Ask the students to write a letter to a student who might be considering this training. In the letter include the following:
- How have you personally grown from this training?
- What new understandings or self-awareness have you gained?
- How might this training change your life?
- How might the skills you've learned here affect your life choices?
- Do you have any recommendations to make to this student about getting the most out of the training?
- Looking back to when you started, what assets have you developed as a result of this training?
- What assets have been strengthened in your own life?
- Are there any other thoughts you might want to share with this student?

Sharing Observations

Go around the group and ask members to reveal whom they have been observing over the course of the training. Ask all group members to share changes in growth and participation they noticed in the student they were observing. When all have finished, ask what effect knowing a group member was observing them may have had on their behavior. Did some members figure out who was observing them, and if so, how? Allow for any further comments.

Evaluation Forms

Ask the group to complete the Training Evaluation Form you have prepared (Handout 25). Students do not have to put their names on these evaluations.

Commitment Postcards

Give each student a postcard. Have the group members address the card to themselves and write a commitment on the card stating how they are going to build assets for and with their peers. They can state this as a goal they want to attain, and they can choose an idea for building assets from the list handed out earlier.

IDENTIFYING ASSETS GAME

Tell the group that they are going to play a game to see how many of the 40 developmental assets they can identify by specific actions. The one who identifies the most correctly will win a prize. In preparation for this game, have group members study their list of the 40 assets (Handout 1) for 10 minutes. Then have students put away their list. Give each student a copy of Handout 26, A List of the 40 Assets without Definitions. Tell students they can use this list for reference.

When ready, distribute Handout 27, Identifying Assets Game. Have the students try to identify which asset each of the actions represents. Some actions could apply to several assets, although each is written to represent a specific asset.

When group members have finished, have them exchange papers and correct them as you read the answers. Give one point for each correct answer. If a student indicates several assets for a particular action or an asset that is not the correct answer, but he or she can make a case supporting the choice, give a full-point credit for it. You can give the student(s) who identified the most assets correctly a prize, such as a copy of *What Teens Need to Succeed.*

Discuss the assets missed the most and those most often identified correctly. Ask group members if they see any pattern in these results. Are some assets less under their control or is less attention given to them? Explain that assets missed the most in this game might be those not explicitly covered in the training. Also state that external assets usually require people in the environment to help a young person develop them. Internal assets are ones young people can more easily develop themselves. Remind students that they can be influential in getting parents, school staff, neighbors, and other community members to be aware of the 40 developmental assets and to take action to help all young people experience them. Ask: What could you do to implement the assets in your work as a peer helper?

RECOGNITION OF TRAINING COMPLETION

It would be significant to give each person some recognition for completing the training successfully. One idea—if there is a budget to allow this—is to give each student a T-shirt with PEER HELPER printed on it. Another idea is to ask a print shop to make business cards for each student (or make them yourself on a computer), with her or his name and PEER HELPER on them, so that the student can pass them out, when appropriate, to other students. These are just suggestions. At the least, you could give group members certificates of completion.

Thank the students for their involvement in the training and commitment to asset building. Indicate that you have benefited from participating in this process with them.

Notes for Leaders

1. The purpose of the evaluation letter to another student is to have group members reflect on their own growth and to help them realize what they have learned.

2. Give plenty of time for the sharing of group member observations. These observations are usually positive and uplifting for everyone.

3. The evaluation form is for the leader's benefit, but it also helps students review and reflect on their training.

4. After two months, mail the postcards to the students. On the postcards, ask them to let you know if they have met their goals or to give you information on how they are using their training. This will yield good evaluation data.

5. An alternative option for playing the Identifying Assets Game might be to set up a game show with groups of participants. Read one action, then give a team 15 seconds to name the asset. If there is no answer or the answer is wrong, the other team gets a chance.

6. If you are working in a school setting (middle school) in which it is not appropriate to talk about sexuality, replace situation 16 on Handout 27 with a different scenario that relates to restraint.

Training Evaluation

- How did this training meet your expectations?

- Which skills did you think were the most valuable?

- What activities (learning experiences) were most useful?

- Which activities were the least useful?

- How helpful/useful was the thought card activity?

- What did you learn about leadership from the training?

- How helpful were the homework assignments?

- What did you learn about building assets for yourself?

- What suggestions would you make to improve this training?

- Other comments you'd like to make:

A List of the 40 Assets without Definitions

Support
1. Family support
2. Positive family communication
3. Other adult relationships
4. Caring neighborhood
5. Caring school climate
6. Parent involvement in schooling

Empowerment
7. Community values youth
8. Youth as resources
9. Service to others
10. Safety

Boundaries and Expectations
11. Family boundaries
12. School boundaries
13. Neighborhood boundaries
14. Adult role models
15. Positive peer influence
16. High expectations

Constructive Use of Time
17. Creative activities
18. Youth programs
19. Religious community
20. Time at home

Commitment to Learning
21. Achievement motivation
22. School engagement
23. Homework
24. Bonding to school
25. Reading for pleasure

Positive Values
26. Caring
27. Equality and social justice
28. Integrity
29. Honesty
30. Responsibility
31. Restraint

Social Competencies
32. Planning and decision making
33. Interpersonal competence
34. Cultural competence
35. Resistance skills
36. Peaceful conflict resolution

Positive Identity
37. Personal power
38. Self-esteem
39. Sense of purpose
40. Positive view of personal future

Identifying Assets Game

Try to identify which asset each of the actions represents. Some actions could apply to several assets, although each is written to represent a specific asset.

ACTIONS	ASSET
1. Parents start an after-school tutoring program where students can get extra help with different subjects.	
2. Students from a predominately Black school and students from a predominately White school spend a day at each of the schools, discussing diversity issues and participating in normal school activities.	
3. Peer helpers gather to discuss what positive things they have learned from their friends and how this has helped them.	
4. You train to be a peer mediator and teach these skills to middle school students.	
5. Peter realizes he hasn't been charged for the carton of soda he has on the bottom of his grocery cart. He goes back and reports it.	
6. You are bored in your ancient history class, so you search the Internet after school for more interesting information on the topics you are studying to get you more involved in the class.	
7. Your family establishes the tradition of having a weekly family dinner together. Everyone takes turns planning and preparing meals.	
8. Your teacher asks each member of the class to recommend a free cultural place or event he or she would like to see or attend. Class trips are planned on the basis of the students' ideas.	

9. For his college application essay, Tim writes about the person he expects to be as an adult and the good things he anticipates doing and achieving before he retires.

10. A student group starts a Caring Student Award to be given to two seniors who are considered to have done the most to reduce cliques and to reach out to students from all groups on campus.

11. Students work on a "map of the community" to identify resources that address social issues and additional services that might be needed.

12. Brenda keeps a daily record of the things she feels good about. When she's feeling down about herself, she goes to her list to remind herself of the good things she has done.

13. Students petition the local newspaper to let them write a weekly column about the positive things youth are doing in the community.

14. The neighborhood organizes a monthly potluck to gather at different homes to discuss neighborhood concerns and desired behaviors.

15. A church youth group plans a series of presentations on different faiths in the community. Each member is urged to invite a classmate to attend.

16. When your boyfriend or girlfriend starts pushing for a sexual relationship, you discuss this with a trusted adult friend and then talk to your boyfriend or girlfriend about the limits you want to set.

17. Your teacher assigns an essay on what you would like to do to improve society and to say what talents or abilities you think you have to help achieve these goals or dreams.

18. You begin asking your parents or guardian about their family experiences when they were growing up.

19. Students in the Friendship Club are matched with incoming students to introduce them to the school's sports, clubs, organizations, and extracurricular activities and to accompany the new students on a visit to one or more of them.

20. Your friend's grades are low. You offer to study with him several nights a week. You give help when needed while you do your own studying.

21. Peer helpers use one of their semester elective classes to serve as aides in the school's classes for students with mental and physical disabilities.

22. When Susan gets uptight and irritable, she takes a Saturday off for a long walk alone or a vigorous bike ride to clear her mind, think through priorities, and return refreshed.

23. The city council establishes a youth committee to discuss youth needs and to work with the council on issues.

24. You ask your parents to agree to a weekly family council to discuss rules, expectations, and activity schedules.

25. You are getting low grades in math. You decide to cut back on your hours at your part-time job and instead locate a tutor to work with you during the extra time.

26. Your father promises you a college tour in the region if all your school work is up-to-date before you leave. You have a term paper due before that time. You work out a plan for getting it finished.

27. Liz sees a new girl standing in the office. She stops, goes up to her, and introduces herself. Then she asks if she can meet her for lunch and introduce her to some of Liz's friends.

28. Peer helpers talk to younger students about the power of negative peer pressure in getting them to do things that could negatively affect their lives.

29. You organize a petition to have more lights installed in your school's parking lot for games and other night events and present this to the school board.

30. A teacher challenges her class to plan, raise money, budget, and execute a spring break camping trip.

31. A teacher invites authors and bookstore employees to speak at his class about books students might like to read. He also takes classes to the library to pick out a book to read aloud and share with the class.

32. A teacher asks students to nominate state/provincial, local, or national politicians whom they admire for the stands they take on issues affecting society. Then the students are asked to discuss why they admire these people.

33. Your class conducts a survey of how students feel about their school. The class develops a project to address some of the concerns expressed on the survey.

34. A group of peer helpers volunteers to work with students who are disruptive or frequently in trouble at school.

35. A family decides to use one night of the weekend as a family fun night at home. Each member takes a turn deciding what the family will do for fun that week.

36. You ask a neighbor who is a scientist to help you out on a science project.

37. A teacher invites respected members of the community to speak to the class about their careers, values, and goals. Students can suggest people to be invited.

38. You start a neighborhood newsletter and interview neighbors about news events and neighborhood needs to write about.

39. You volunteer to be a regular visitor at the retirement home in your community.

40. John agrees to be home from a party at 11 P.M. When someone needs a ride that would make him late, he calls his parents to explain.

Answers for Identifying Assets

ACTIONS	ASSET AND NUMBER	
1	Parent involvement in schooling	#6
2	Cultural competence	#34
3	Positive peer influence	#15
4	Peaceful conflict resolution	#36
5	Honesty	#29
6	School engagement	#22
7	Family support	#1
8	Creative activities	#17
9	Positive view of personal future	#40
10	Bonding to school	#24
11	Equality and social justice	#27
12	Self-esteem	#38
13	Youth as resources	#8
14	Neighborhood boundaries	#13
15	Religious community	#19
16	Restraint	#31
17	Sense of purpose	#39
18	Positive family communication	#2
19	Youth programs	#18
20	Homework	#23
21	Caring	#26
22	Personal power	#37

23	Community values youth	#7
24	Family boundaries	#11
25	Achievement motivation	#21
26	Planning and decision making	#32
27	Interpersonal competence	#33
28	Resistance skills	#35
29	Safety	#10
30	High expectations	#16
31	Reading for pleasure	#25
32	Integrity	#28
33	Caring school climate	#5
34	School boundaries	#12
35	Time at home	#20
36	Other adult relationships	#3
37	Adult role models	#14
38	Caring neighborhood	#4
39	Service to others	#9
40	Responsibility	#30

Appendixes

The mission of the National Peer Helpers Association (now a part of Search Institute) is to equip individuals to help others by promoting standards of excellence in peer programs. You may want to set up and manage your peer-helping program in alignment with the association's *Programmatic Standards and Ethics,* which are included here for your convenience.

National Peer Helpers Assocation
Programmatic Standards Checklist

I. PROGRAM START-UP

A. Planning
- ☐ Rationale based on needs assessment
- ☐ Purpose
- ☐ Goals and Objectives
- ☐ Procedures
- ☐ Compliance

B. Commitment
- ☐ Administrative and Community Support
- ☐ Program Advisory Committee
- ☐ Resources

C. Staffing
- ☐ Positive rapport with peer helpers
- ☐ Continuing education and experience relevant to program goals
- ☐ Commitment to the fundamental principles of peer helping
- ☐ Familiarity with the program setting
- ☐ Clear understanding of the program needs and goals
- ☐ Ability to articulate goals to peer helpers, staff, sponsors, and community
- ☐ Skills necessary for training and supervision
- ☐ Time to train, plan, evaluate, and supervise

D. Organizational Structure
- ☐ Clear lines of authority, responsibility, and communication
- ☐ Reflects the nature and purpose of the program

II. PROGRAM IMPLEMENTATION

A. Screening and Selection
- ☐ Establish criteria for peer helpers
- ☐ Conduct a formal or informal survey to identify potential helpers
- ☐ Establish application procedures
- ☐ Employ selection guidelines such as:
  - ➤ Demonstration of appropriate helping characteristics and skills
  - ➤ Demonstration of emotional security/stability
  - ➤ Understanding of services to be provided
  - ➤ Commitment to providing services
  - ➤ Sensitivity to population being served
  - ➤ Demonstration of the ability to follow through over time
  - ➤ Manageability of group size for training and supervision

B. Training

Training Characteristics:

- ☐ Reflects nature and goals of program
- ☐ Takes into account age, needs, and characteristics of population served
- ☐ Utilizes appropriate curricular resources and training strategies
- ☐ Is consistent with guidelines regarding standards and ethics
- ☐ Includes demonstration, skill development, practice, and critique
- ☐ Provides specialized training for specific services
- ☐ Remains ongoing

Training Elements:

- ☐ Role of the Peer Helper
- ☐ Confidentiality/Liability Issues
- ☐ Communication Skills
- ☐ Problem-Solving/Decision-Making Strategies
- ☐ Additional Issues and Topics Relevant to Particular Program

C. Service Delivery

- ☐ Appropriate variety of meaningful, productive helping roles within the program

D. Supervision

- ☐ Regular and ongoing supervision

III. PROGRAM MAINTENANCE

A. Evaluation

- ☐ Process Evaluation
- ☐ Impact Evaluation
- ☐ Outcomes
- ☐ Cost Benefit

B. Public Relations

- ☐ Well-informed external and internal supporters and potential program recipients
- ☐ Program brochure or newsletter
- ☐ Media contacts

C. Long-range Planning

- ☐ Staffing
- ☐ Peer ownership
- ☐ Funding

Programmatic Standards
National Peer Helpers Association

The National Peer Helpers Association believes the following standards are essential for any quality peer program.

I. PROGRAM START-UP

A. Planning

Prior to program implementation, the following issues must be addressed through careful planning:

1. Rationale: There is a clear and compelling rationale for the development of the program; frequently, this is accomplished through conducting a formal or informal needs assessment in the setting in which the program is to be implemented.
2. Purpose: Based on the rationale, the purpose of the program must be conveyed through a formal mission statement.
3. Goals and Objectives: Programmatic goals and objectives (a) reflect the rationale and purpose of the program; and (b) are clear, measurable, and achievable.
4. Procedures: Programmatic goals are accomplished through procedures and activities that are laid out in a clear and systematic fashion.
5. Compliance: The program is planned and implemented in a manner consistent with local, state, and national guidelines for programmatic standards and ethics (see *NPHA Code of Ethics for Peer Helping Professionals and Peer Helpers* on pages 157–158).

B. Commitment

The program will expect the active commitment and involvement of those who are directly involved. Commitment is reflected in the following areas:

1. Evidence of a high level of administrative, staff, and community support; in many cases, this includes the formation of a program advisory committee.
2. Advisory committee members may or may not be directly involved in program implementation. They provide a valuable link to the community and give input to program staff in order to maximize a sense of program ownership. They also sustain the program to enable it to survive changes in administration and program staff.
3. Sufficient financial and logistical support for effective program implementation is optimal; such support includes the provision of necessary curricular and training resources. (Please note that programs can be implemented without a high level of administrative/staff/community support and with a minimum of financial support. However, that support would ideally come later.)

C. Staffing

Program staff should possess the appropriate background, training, and characteristics to enable them to carry out their responsibilities in an effective and ethical manner. The following skills are essential for professional staff who work directly with peer helpers:

1. A positive rapport with the population from which the peer helpers are selected.
2. Continuing educational and practical experience that is relevant to the goals of the program.
3. Understanding of, and commitment to, the fundamental principles of peer helping, with emphasis on maintaining peer helpers' ownership and involvement in the program.
4. Familiarity with the setting in which the program is to be implemented, such as in a school, community, or faith-based organization.

5. Clear understanding of the program's needs and goals and an ability to effectively articulate the nature and purpose of the program to peer helpers, other staff, the sponsoring agency, and the broader community.

D. Organizational Structure

The program should be organized and structured in a logical and consistent manner that provides clear lines of authority, responsibility, and communication. The structure also should reflect the nature and purpose of the program.

II. PROGRAM IMPLEMENTATION

A. Screening and Selection

The program should employ a clear, systematic, and careful procedure for the screening and selection of peer helpers. Typically, this procedure includes the following:

1. Establishing appropriate criteria as to the characteristics being sought among prospective peer helpers. Among those characteristics are helpfulness, trustworthiness, concern for others, ability to listen, and potential to serve as a positive role model.
2. Conducting a formal or informal survey in the program setting, in order to determine which individuals are felt to possess the desired characteristics.
3. Making application to the program, soliciting recommendations from others in the program setting, and structuring an interview with program staff. The interview should include samples of the type of skills required of the peer helper, e.g. public presentations, phone skills, and meeting new people.

Programs may differ as to whether final selection of peer helpers should occur prior to or after peer-helper training. In either case, the selection process should be guided by the following criteria:

1. Demonstration of appropriate helping characteristics and skills.
2. Evidence of emotional security/stability.
3. Understanding of the type(s) of services to be provided.
4. Commitment to and availability for the provision of those services.
5. Ability to be reflective of and sensitive to the characteristics of the population to be served.
6. Demonstration of the ability to follow through over time.
7. Manageability of the size of the group selected, in order to ensure quality training and supervision.

B. Training

Once peer helpers have been selected, they should be provided with quality training in the knowledge and skills they will need to be effective as peer helpers. The training program that is implemented should do the following: (a) be reflective of the nature and goals of the program; (b) take into account the age, needs, and characteristics of the population to be served; (c) utilize appropriate curricular resources and training strategies; and (d) be consistent with local, state, and national guidelines on ethics and standards. All training should include demonstration, skill development, practice, and critique. Additional training is necessary to provide specific services as described in #5 below. Trainees should commit to participate in all aspects of training and to maximize opportunities for both skill development and personal growth. Finally, training should be viewed as an ongoing process, one that is never completed.

While specific features of training may vary somewhat from program to program, the following elements are characteristic of effective peer-helping training models:

1. *Role of the Peer Helper*

   Training in the peer-helping role includes, but is not be limited to, the following:
   a. Program orientation.
   b. Characteristics of the helper (caring, acceptance, genuineness, understanding, trustworthiness).
   c. Self-awareness.
   d. Positive role-modeling; e.g., maintaining a healthy lifestyle.
   e. Avoidance of temptation to offer advice, propose solutions, or impose values.
   f. Positive listening skills.
   g. Recognition of limitations.
   h. Developing of individual and group trust.
   i. Creation of a support system of peer helpers for each other, as well as for helpees.
   j. Development of a code of ethics and standards of behavior.

2. *Confidentiality/Liability Issues*

   While communications between peer helpers and helpees are typically confidential, there are 3 important exceptions to this general rule:
   a. Stated or implied threats to the personal safety or well-being of the peer helper, helpee, or others.
   b. Child abuse, sexual abuse, family dysfunction, psychotic behavior, harm to self and others, and drug and alcohol abuse.
   c. Situations or problems beyond the personal expertise of the peer helper. An essential component of any peer-helping training program is that peer helpers know how to recognize such situations, are aware of their limitations and responsibilities, and have ready access to professional staff and appropriate referral resources.

3. *Communication Skills*

   Effective peer helping requires the use of the following:
   a. Basic principles of verbal and nonverbal communication.
   b. Active listening skills (attending, empathizing, etc.).
   c. Facilitative responding (questioning, clarifying, summarizing, etc.).
   d. Skills for communicating in a diverse situation (meeting new students, conversing with students from different countries and cultures, etc.).

4. *Problem-Solving/Decision-Making Strategies*

   Effective peer helping often involves the use of steps in formal problem solving (identifying the problem; brainstorming alternatives; predicting consequences; carrying out action plan; evaluating results).

5. *Additional Issues and Topics*

   Depending upon the nature and goals of particular programs, additional specialized training may be provided in areas such as the following:
   a. Basic concepts of human behavior. Peer helpers should have some degree of familiarity with concepts such as the following:
      1. The role of motivational and reinforcement factors in behavior.
      2. Sociocultural influences and differences.
      3. Individual and group dynamics.
   b. Group facilitation techniques.
   c. Learning styles and teaching strategies.
   d. Peer tutoring strategies.
   e. Crisis management.
   f. Conflict resolution, mediation, and anger management.

g. Special needs populations.

h. Telephone "hotline" management.

i. Specific problem areas (substance abuse, dropouts, depression, suicide, teen pregnancy, child abuse, sexually transmitted diseases, gangs and cults, family relations, etc.).

j. Knowledge of referral resources, services, and programs.

C. Service Delivery

Subsequent to training, peer helpers should be provided with structured opportunities to engage in a variety of meaningful, productive helping roles within the program setting. The peer-helping services provided should:

1. Be consistent with and reflective of program goals.
2. Enable peer helpers to apply the knowledge and skills they have acquired during training.
3. Enhance the personal growth and positive development of peer helpers and helpees alike.
4. Recognize and accommodate the need for ongoing opportunities for continued learning and training.

D. Supervision

Once peer helpers have begun to provide services, it is imperative that they receive regular, ongoing supervision from program staff. In addition to regularly scheduled sessions, staff should be available to provide supplemental supervision and support as needed. Major goals of supervision include the following:

1. Enable program staff to monitor program-related activities and services.
2. Enhance the effectiveness and personal growth of peer helpers.
3. Encourage peer helpers to share with, learn from, and support each other in the performance of their helping roles.
4. Establish safeguards to protect peer helpers from too many program responsibilities, role confusion, or inappropriate assignments.

III. PROGRAM MAINTENANCE

Once the program has been established, program staff should take steps to ensure its continued sustainment, improvement, success, and expansion or infusion into a system. These steps include the following:

A. Evaluation

Evaluation is conducted to document program-related activities and services. It is done to assess the process, impact, outcome, and cost benefits of the program with reference to its mission, goals, and objectives. The program should develop and implement a formal evaluation plan. Evaluation data should be utilized to examine program effectiveness and to determine whether and how the program needs to be revised. The evaluation plan may include four components:

1. Process Evaluation

   Process evaluation provides a picture of what happened in connection with the program and its consistency with *NPHA Programmatic Standards*. Process evaluation determines the degree to which the program has been successful in achieving its goals and objectives aligned with the mission. Process data includes information in such areas as number of peer helpers and helpees involved; program staffing and organization; selection procedures; nature and extent of training; amount and types of services provided; and other program-related activities.

2. Impact Evaluation

   Impact evaluation typically assesses the effect of the program upon both peer helpers and those who have received program services within a set period of time. Such assessment can be qualitative (open-ended questionnaires, opinion surveys, etc.) and/or can employ quantitative indices of program impact. In a school-based program, for example, impact evaluation might assess effectiveness in such areas as student knowledge, attitudes, beliefs, and skills or behaviors (e.g., grade point average, absenteeism and dropout rates, or incidence of disciplinary referrals).

3. Outcomes

   Outcome evaluation assesses long-term changes to the peer helper, those they serve, and the community. Examples of societal benefits are fewer alcohol-related crashes and deaths, employment, improved leadership skills, and lower health risk parameters.

4. Cost Benefit

   Costs benefits are the monetary savings related to the effectiveness of the program (e.g., the cost of the program in providing services to at-risk students, thus reducing dropout rates which will increase A.D.A. funds to the school).

B. Public Relations

Program staff should make a concerted, ongoing effort to keep external and internal supporters and potential program recipients informed about the benefits and accomplishments of the program. Informative techniques might include brochures, presentations, newsletters, and media communication.

C. Long-Range Planning

Program staff should engage in long-range planning to ensure that the program is sustained and infused. Key factors to consider in long-range planning include the following:

1. Staffing: The success of the program is dependent on a broad-based ownership. This can be accomplished by having a planning team, advisory committee, and multiple staff participation. At least one individual within the program setting should be prepared in coordination responsibilities in the event of staffing changes.

2. Peer Ownership: The program should maximize the level of ownership and involvement of peer helpers. When peer helpers feel directly responsible for the success and sustainment of the program, the program is more likely to be infused.

3. Funding: The program should have a secure and consistent funding base. There need to be contingency plans to provide for continued operation in the event of reduced or nonexistent funding.

National Peer Helpers Association Code of Ethics
For Peer Helping Professionals

Professionals who are responsible for implementing peer-helping programs shall be people of personal and professional integrity. To be ethical, peer professionals must operate programs in alignment with NPHA Programmatic Standards. NPHA believes the Code of Ethics for Peer Helping Professionals should contain the following guidelines:

1. A belief that peer helping is an effective way to address the needs and conditions of people.
2. A commitment to an individual's right to dignity, self-development, and self-direction.
3. Program development and implementation which demonstrates:
   - A strong positive rapport with peer helpers.
   - Personal commitment to the peer-helping program.
   - Integrity of acquiring necessary training for specific work with students (e.g., tutoring, mediation, etc.).
   - Utilization of a training curriculum that is aligned with *NPHA Programmatic Standards.*
4. Selection of trainers and program managers who:
   - Model positive behavior.
   - Reject the pursuit of personal power or gain at the expense of others.
   - Respect copyright and acknowledgment obligations.
   - Adhere to the ethics and legalities of confidential issues (abuse and harm to self and others).

National Peer Helpers Association Code of Ethics
For Peer Helpers

A CODE OF ETHICS IS AN AGREEMENT AMONG THOSE WHO COMMIT TO THE PROGRAM AS TO THE NORMS THAT SHALL GUIDE THEIR BEHAVIOR DURING THEIR INVOLVEMENT IN THE PROGRAM.

Peer helpers shall be people of personal integrity. NPHA believes peer helpers will:

1. Embrace the philosophy that peer helping is an effective way to address the needs and conditions of people.
2. Respect the individual's right to dignity, self-development, and self-direction.
3. Model positive behaviors and life choices (e.g., no substance use/abuse).
4. Embrace the concept of service to others for the good of the community.
5. Maintain confidentiality of information imparted during the course of program related activities with the exceptions of child abuse, sexual abuse, family dysfunction, psychotic behavior, harm to self and others, and drug and alcohol abuse.
6. Refrain from tackling situations for which they have no training and preparation (e.g., peer mediation, tutoring, etc.).
7. Recognize, report, and know techniques to deal with stated or implied threats to their emotional or physical well-being.